CW01560361

COMPANY LAW MATERIALS
1997

COMPANY LAW MATERIALS 1997

Editor

Peter G Van Duzer LLB, Solicitor

JORDANS

1997

Published by
Jordan Publishing Limited
21 St Thomas Street
Bristol BS1 6JS

© Jordan Publishing Limited 1997
Reprinted August 1998
Reprinted September 1999
Reprinted August 2000

British Library Cataloguing-in-Publication Data
A catalogue record for this book is available from the British Library.

ISSN 1360–2470
ISBN 0 85308 442 4

Typeset by Mendip Communications Limited, Frome
Printed in Great Britain by Hobbs The Printers of Southampton

PREFACE

This book is intended to illustrate the documentation required for the incorporation of a private limited company and to be filed on subsequent occasions in the circumstances specified in the Companies Act 1985, as amended as at 30 April 1997. Part 4 also refers to and illustrates some of the principal documentation required to be filed by a foreign company which establishes a place of business or a branch in Great Britain in accordance with requirements, as at 30 April 1997.

The forms for filing at Companies House accord with the requirements of Statutory Instruments in force as at 30 April 1997.

Form numbers prefixed by the letter 'J' are Jordans copyright drafts for which no official format has been prescribed.

The specimen draft Memorandum and Articles of Association extend the regulations contained in Tables A and B applicable to the Companies Act 1985 and, in particular, adjust Table A (Articles of Association) to the needs of a private limited company. They have recently been settled by Counsel (Mr Richard Sykes QC and Mr Andrew Thornton, of Lincoln's Inn) in the light of current law and practice. Various other alternative clauses are provided in relation to the transfer of shares and other points. The specimen draft makes use of the statement of a company's objects for a general commercial company, provided for by section 3A of the Companies Act 1985. Different wording at the start and end of clause 3 of the Memorandum will be required if specific objects are to be used. More detailed comment on this is set out in the commentary.

Tables A and B are prescribed by the Companies (Tables A to F) Regulations 1985 (SI 1985 No 805) as amended by the Companies (Tables A to F) (Amendment) Regulations 1985 (SI 1985 No 1052). These Tables A and B came into operation on 1 July 1985, subject to minor changes effective from 1 August 1985. There are still many older companies using Articles based on Table A as prescribed in the previous Companies Act 1948 or by earlier legislation and it should be noted that the 1985 Table A contains substantial changes from that under the 1948 Act.

CONTENTS

4

3. ADMINISTRATIVE RECORDS OF A PRIVATE LIMITED COMPANY

Introduction to and Specimens of:

4. DOCUMENTS TO BE FILED AT THE COMPANIES REGISTRY IN RESPECT OF A FOREIGN COMPANY WHICH ESTABLISHES A PLACE OF BUSINESS OR A BRANCH IN GREAT BRITAIN

6

1. DOCUMENTS LEADING TO THE INCORPORATION OF A PRIVATE LIMITED COMPANY HAVING A SHARE CAPITAL

(This section is on pages 9 to 79. Contents are listed on page 3.)

Introduction

Memorandum and Articles of Association (sections 1 to 9 and Tables A and B). The Memorandum of Association and the Articles of Association are, in fact, two separate documents. However, they are usually bound together as if one document and referred to as 'Memorandum and Articles of Association'. In this case, we have included a Memorandum making use of the general commercial object and (for illustration) the first page only of a Memorandum using a specific object (see notes). Article 1 of the specimen Articles of Association adopts the prescribed model set of regulations known as 'Table A' with the additions and modifications set out in the rest of the Articles of Association. Therefore, Table A is also printed in full. Various optional additional or alternative Articles have also been set out.

First directors and secretary and intended situation of registered office – Form 10 (section 10). Each director and secretary must sign the "consent to act" portion of the Form, which must also be signed by or on behalf of the subscribers.

Declaration on application for registration – Form 12 (section 12(3)). This must be sworn by a solicitor engaged in the formation of the company or a person named as Director or Secretary of the company on the Form 10.

Note: Although relevant principally to companies limited by guarantee, we have included at the end of this part Forms 30(5)(a), 30(5)(b) and 30(5)(c). The sections permit exemption from the requirement to use the word "limited" or its Welsh equivalent in the company name if the objects of the company are, or are to be, the promotion of commerce, art, science, education, religion, charity or any profession and anything incidental or conducive to those objects, and also if the Memorandum or Articles of Association require the profits or other income to be applied in promoting its objects, prohibit the payment of dividends to the members, and require all assets otherwise available to members on a winding up to be transferred to a body with similar objects or to a body the objects of which are the promotion of charity and anything incidental or conducive thereto. Form 30(5)(a) is the form appropriate for use on incorporation of a company limited by guarantee.

STANDARD

MEMORANDUM AND ARTICLES OF

ASSOCIATION

FOR

A PRIVATE COMPANY LIMITED BY SHARES

as re-settled for
JORDANS LIMITED
by
Richard Sykes QC and Andrew Thornton
of
Erskine Chambers, Lincoln's Inn

27 June 1997

MEMORANDUM OF ASSOCIATION
[with general commercial object clause]

THE COMPANIES ACTS 1985 to 1989

PRIVATE COMPANY LIMITED BY SHARES

MEMORANDUM OF ASSOCIATION OF

[With general commercial object clause pursuant to section 3A of the Companies Act 1985]

●　　●　　　　**LIMITED**

1.　　　　The Company's name is " ●　　●　　　**LIMITED**".

2.　　　　The Company's registered office is to be situated in England and Wales.

3.1　　　The object of the Company is to carry on business as a general commercial company.

3.2　　　Without prejudice to the generality of the object and the powers of the Company derived from Section 3A of the Act the Company has power to do all or any of the following things:-

3.2.1　　To purchase or by any other means acquire and take options over any property whatever, and any rights or privileges of any kind over or in respect of any property.

3.2.2 To apply for, register, purchase, or by other means acquire and protect, prolong and renew, whether in the United Kingdom or elsewhere, any trade marks, patents, copyrights, trade secrets, or other intellectual property rights, licences, secret processes, designs, protections and concessions and to disclaim, alter, modify, use and turn to account and to manufacture under or grant licences or privileges in respect of the same, and to expend money in experimenting upon, testing and improving any patents, inventions or rights which the Company may acquire or propose to acquire.

3.2.3 To acquire or undertake the whole or any part of the business, goodwill, and assets of any person, firm, or company carrying on or proposing to carry on any of the businesses which the Company is authorised to carry on and as part of the consideration for such acquisition to undertake all or any of the liabilities of such person, firm or company, or to acquire an interest in, amalgamate with, or enter into partnership or into any arrangement for sharing profits, or for co-operation, or for mutual assistance with any such person, firm or company, or for subsidising or otherwise assisting any such person, firm or company, and to give or accept, by way of consideration for any of the acts or things aforesaid or property acquired, any shares, debentures, debenture stock or securities that may be agreed upon, and to hold and retain, or sell, mortgage and deal with any shares, debentures, debenture stock or securities so received.

3.2.4 To improve, manage, construct, repair, develop, exchange, let on lease or otherwise, mortgage, charge, sell, dispose of, turn to account, grant licences, options, rights and privileges in respect of, or otherwise deal with all or any part of the property and rights of the Company.

3.2.5 To invest and deal with the moneys of the Company not immediately required in such manner as may from time to time be determined and to hold or otherwise deal with any investments made.

3.2.6 To lend and advance money or give credit on any terms and with or without security to any person, firm or company (including without prejudice to the generality of the foregoing any holding company, subsidiary or fellow subsidiary of, or any other company associated in any way with, the Company), to enter into guarantees, contracts of indemnity and suretyships of all kinds, to receive money on deposit or loan upon any terms, and to secure or guarantee in any manner and upon any terms the payment of any sum of money or the performance of any obligation by any person, firm or company (including without prejudice to the generality of the foregoing any such holding company, subsidiary, fellow subsidiary or associated company as aforesaid).

3.2.7 To borrow and raise money in any manner and to secure the repayment of any money borrowed, raised or owing by mortgage, charge, standard security, lien or other security upon the whole or any part of the Company's property or assets (whether present or future), including its uncalled capital, and also by a similar mortgage, charge, standard security, lien or security to secure and guarantee the performance by the Company of any obligation or liability it may undertake or which may become binding on it.

3.2.8 To draw, make, accept, endorse, discount, negotiate, execute and issue cheques, bills of exchange, promissory notes, bills of lading, warrants, debentures, and other negotiable or transferable instruments.

3.2.9 To apply for, promote, and obtain any Act of Parliament, order, or licence of the Department of Trade or other authority for enabling the Company to carry any of its objects into effect, or for effecting any modification of the Company's constitution, or for any other purpose which may seem calculated directly or indirectly to promote the Company's interests, and to oppose any proceedings or applications which may seem calculated directly or indirectly to prejudice the Company's interests.

3.2.10 To enter into any arrangements with any government or authority (supreme, municipal, local, or otherwise) that may seem conducive to the attainment of the Company's objects or any of them, and to obtain from any such government or authority any charters, decrees, rights, privileges or concessions which the Company may think desirable and to carry out, exercise, and comply with any such charters, decrees, rights, privileges, and concessions.

3.2.11 To subscribe for, take, purchase, or otherwise acquire, hold, sell, deal with and dispose of, place and underwrite shares, stocks, debentures, debenture stocks, bonds, obligations or securities issued or guaranteed by any other company constituted or carrying on business in any part of the world, and debentures, debenture stocks, bonds, obligations or securities issued or guaranteed by any government or authority, municipal, local or otherwise, in any part of the world.

3.2.12 To control, manage, finance, subsidise, co-ordinate or otherwise assist any company or companies in which the Company has a direct or indirect financial interest, to provide secretarial, administrative, technical, commercial and other services and facilities of all kinds for any such company or companies and to make payments by way of subvention or otherwise and any other arrangements which may seem desirable with respect to any business or operations of or generally with respect to any such company or companies.

3.2.13 To promote any other company for the purpose of acquiring the whole or any part of the business or property or undertaking or any of the liabilities of the Company, or of undertaking any business or operations which may appear likely to assist or benefit the Company or to enhance the value of any property or business of the Company, and to place or guarantee the placing of, underwrite, subscribe for, or otherwise acquire all or any part of the shares or securities of any such company as aforesaid.

3.2.14 To sell or otherwise dispose of the whole or any part of the business or property of the Company, either together or in portions, for such consideration as the Company may think fit, and in particular for shares, debentures, or securities of any company purchasing the same.

3.2.15 To act as agents or brokers and as trustees for any person, firm or company, and to undertake and perform sub-contracts.

3.2.16 To remunerate any person, firm or company rendering services to the Company either by cash payment or by the allotment of shares or other securities of the Company credited as paid up in full or in part or otherwise as may be thought expedient.

3.2.17 To distribute among the members of the Company in kind any property of the Company of whatever nature.

3.2.18 To pay all or any expenses incurred in connection with the promotion, formation and incorporation of the Company, or to contract with any person, firm or company to pay the same, and to pay commissions to brokers and others for underwriting, placing, selling, or guaranteeing the subscription of any shares or other securities of the Company.

3.2.19 To support and subscribe to any charitable or public object and to support and subscribe to any institution, society, or club which may be for the benefit of the Company or its directors or employees, or may be connected with any town or place where the Company carries on business; to give or award pensions, annuities, gratuities, and superannuation or other allowances or benefits or charitable aid and generally to provide advantages, facilities and services for any persons who are or have been directors of, or who are or have been employed by, or who are serving or have served the Company, or any company which is a subsidiary of the Company or the holding company of the Company or a fellow subsidiary of the Company or the predecessors in business of the Company or of any such subsidiary, holding or fellow subsidiary company and to the wives, widows, children and other relatives and dependants of such persons; to make payments towards insurance including insurance for any director, officer or auditor against any liability in respect of any negligence, default, breach of duty or breach of trust (so far as permitted by law); and to set up, establish, support and maintain superannuation and other funds or schemes (whether contributory or non-contributory) for the benefit of any of such persons and of their wives, widows, children and other relatives and dependants; and to set up, establish, support and maintain profit sharing or share purchase schemes for the benefit of any of the employees of the Company or of any such subsidiary, holding or fellow subsidiary company and to lend money to any such employees or to trustees on their behalf to enable any such schemes to be established or maintained.

3.2.20 Subject to and in accordance with the provisions of the Act (if and so far as such provisions shall be applicable) to give, directly or indirectly, financial assistance for the acquisition of shares or other securities of the Company or of any other company or for the reduction or discharge of any liability incurred in respect of such acquisition.

3.2.21 To procure the Company to be registered or recognised in any part of the world.

3.2.22 To do all or any of the things or matters aforesaid in any part of the world and either as principals, agents, contractors or otherwise, and by or through agents, brokers, sub-contractors or otherwise and either alone or in conjunction with others.

3.2.23 To do all such other things as may be deemed incidental or conducive to the attainment of the Company's objects or any of them.

3.2.24 AND so that:–

3.2.24.1 None of the provisions set forth in any sub-clause of this clause shall be restrictively construed but the widest interpretation shall be given to each such provision, and none of such provisions shall, except where the context expressly so requires, be in any way limited or restricted by reference to or inference from any other provision set forth in such sub-clause, or by reference to or inference from the terms of any other sub-clause of this clause, or by reference to or inference from the name of the Company.

3.2.24.2   The word "company" in this clause, except where used in reference to the Company, shall be deemed to include any partnership or other body of persons, whether incorporated or unincorporated and whether domiciled in the United Kingdom or elsewhere.

3.2.24.3   In this clause the expression "the Act" means the Companies Act 1985, but so that any reference in this clause to any provision of the Act shall be deemed to include a reference to any statutory modification or re-enactment of that provision for the time being in force.

4.   The liability of the members is limited.

5.   The Company's share capital is £● divided into ● shares of £● each.

MEMORANDUM OF ASSOCIATION
[with specific object clause, first and last pages only,
see commentary]

THE COMPANIES ACTS 1985 to 1989

PRIVATE COMPANY LIMITED BY SHARES

MEMORANDUM OF ASSOCIATION OF

[With specific objects clause and "Cotman v Brougham" multiple objects]

● ● **LIMITED**

1. The Company's name is " ● ● LIMITED".

2. The Company's registered office is to be situated in England and Wales.

3. The Company's objects are:-

3.1.1 ● ● ●

3.1.2 To carry on any other trade or business whatever which can in the opinion of the board of directors be advantageously carried on in connection with or ancillary to any of the businesses of the Company.

3.2 To purchase or by any other means acquire and take options over any property whatever, and any rights or privileges of any kind over or in respect of any property.

[And continue with clauses 3.2.2 to 3.2.23 inclusive of the general commercial object version as clauses 3.3 to 3.24]

[Different final clause for use with specific objects]

3.25   AND so that:-

3.25.1   None of the objects set forth in any sub-clause of this clause shall be restrictively construed but the widest interpretation shall be given to each such object, and none of such objects shall, except where the context expressly so requires, be in any way limited or restricted by reference to or inference from any other object or objects set forth in such sub-clause, or by reference to or inference from the terms of any other sub-clause of this clause, or by reference to or inference from the name of the Company.

3.25.2   None of the sub-clauses of this clause and none of the objects therein specified shall be deemed subsidiary or ancillary to any of the objects specified in any other such sub-clause, and the Company shall have as full a power to exercise each and every one of the objects specified in each sub-clause of this clause as though each such sub-clause contained the objects of a separate Company.

3.25.3   The word "company" in this clause, except where used in reference to the Company, shall be deemed to include any partnership or other body of persons, whether incorporated or unincorporated and whether domiciled in the United Kingdom or elsewhere.

3.25.4   In this clause the expression "the Act" means the Companies Act 1985, but so that any reference in this clause to any provision of the Act shall be deemed to include a reference to any statutory modification or re-enactment of that provision for the time being in force.

4.   The liability of the members is limited.

5.   The Company's share capital is £● divided into ● shares of £● each.

ARTICLES OF ASSOCIATION

THE COMPANIES ACTS 1985 to 1989

PRIVATE COMPANY LIMITED BY SHARES

ARTICLES OF ASSOCIATION OF

● ● **LIMITED**

1. PRELIMINARY

1.1 The regulations contained in Table A in the Schedule to the Companies (Tables A to F) Regulations 1985 (SI 1985 No. 805) as amended by the Companies (Tables A to F) (Amendment) Regulations 1985 (SI 1985 No. 1052) (such Table being hereinafter called "Table A") shall apply to the Company save in so far as they are excluded or varied hereby and such regulations (save as so excluded or varied) and the Articles hereinafter contained shall be the Articles of Association of the Company.

1.2 In these Articles the expression "the Act" means the Companies Act 1985, but so that any reference in these Articles to any provision of the Act shall be deemed to include a reference to any statutory modification or re-enactment of that provision for the time being in force.

2. ALLOTMENT OF SHARES

2.1 Shares which are comprised in the authorised share capital with which the Company is incorporated shall be under the control of the directors who may (subject to section 80 of the Act and to Article 2.4 below) allot, grant options over or otherwise dispose of the same, to such persons, on such terms and in such manner as they think fit.

2.2 All shares which are not comprised in the authorised share capital with which the Company is incorporated and which the directors propose to issue shall first be offered to the members in proportion as nearly as may be to the number of the existing shares held by them respectively unless the Company in general meeting shall by special resolution otherwise direct. The offer shall be made by notice specifying the number of shares offered, and limiting a period (not being less than 14 days) within which the offer, if not accepted, will be deemed to be declined. After the expiration of that period, those shares so deemed to be declined shall be offered in the proportion aforesaid to the persons who have, within the said period, accepted all the shares offered to them; such further offer shall be made in like terms in the same manner and limited by a like period as the original offer. Any shares not accepted pursuant to such offer or further offer as aforesaid or not capable of being offered as aforesaid except by way of fractions and any shares released from the provisions of this Article by any such special resolution as aforesaid shall be under the control of the directors, who may allot, grant options over or otherwise dispose of the same to such persons, on such terms, and in such manner as they think fit, provided that, in the case of shares not accepted as aforesaid, such shares shall not be disposed of on terms which are more favourable to the subscribers therefor than the terms on which they were offered to the members. The foregoing provisions of this Article 2.2 shall have effect subject to section 80 of the Act.

2.3 In accordance with section 91(1) of the Act sections 89(1) and 90(1) to (6) (inclusive) of the Act shall not apply to the Company.

s.89 does't apply to incorporated share capital only

2.4 The directors are generally and unconditionally authorised for the purposes of section 80 of the Act to exercise any power of the Company to allot and grant rights to subscribe for or convert securities into shares of the Company up to the amount of the authorised share capital with which the Company is incorporated at any time or times during the period of five years from the date of incorporation and the directors may, after that period, allot any shares or grant any such rights under this authority in pursuance of an offer or agreement so to do made by the Company within that period. The authority hereby given may at any time (subject to the said section 80) be renewed, revoked or varied by ordinary resolution.

3. SHARES

3.1 The lien conferred by regulation 8 in Table A shall attach also to fully paid-up shares, and the Company shall also have a first and paramount lien on all shares, whether fully paid or not, standing registered in the name of any person indebted or under liability to the Company, whether he shall be the sole registered holder thereof or shall be one of two or more joint holders, for all moneys presently payable by him or his estate to the Company. Regulation 8 in Table A shall be modified accordingly.

3.2 The liability of any member in default in respect of a call shall be increased by the addition at the end of the first sentence of regulation 18 in Table A of the words "and all expenses that may have been incurred by the Company by reason of such non-payment".

4. GENERAL MEETINGS AND RESOLUTIONS

4.1 Every notice convening a general meeting shall comply with the provisions of section 372(3) of the Act as to giving information to members in regard to their right to appoint proxies; and notices of and other communications relating to any general meeting which any member is entitled to receive shall be sent to the directors and to the auditors for the time being of the Company.

4.2.1 No business shall be transacted at any general meeting unless a quorum is present. Subject to Article 4.2.2 below, two persons entitled to vote upon the business to be transacted, each being a member or a proxy for a member or a duly authorised representative of a corporation, shall be a quorum.

4.2.2 If and for so long as the Company has only one member, that member present in person or by proxy or (if that member is a corporation) by a duly authorised representative shall be a quorum.

4.2.3 If a quorum is not present within half an hour from the time appointed for a general meeting the general meeting shall stand adjourned to the same day in the next week at the same time and place or to such other day and at such other time and place as the directors may determine; and if at the adjourned general meeting a quorum is not present within half an hour from the time appointed therefor such adjourned general meeting shall be dissolved.

4.2.4 Regulations 40 and 41 in Table A shall not apply to the Company.

4.3.1 If and for so long as the Company has only one member and that member takes any decision which is required to be taken in general meeting or by means of a written resolution, that decision shall be as valid and effectual as if agreed by the Company in general meeting, subject as provided in Article 4.3.3 below.

4.3.2 Any decision taken by a sole member pursuant to Article 4.3.1 above shall be recorded in writing and delivered by that member to the Company for entry in the Company's minute book.

4.3.3 Resolutions under section 303 of the Act for the removal of a director before the expiration of his period of office and under section 391 of the Act for the removal of an auditor before the expiration of his period of office shall only be considered by the Company in general meeting.

4.4 A member present at a meeting by proxy shall be entitled to speak at the meeting and shall be entitled to one vote on a show of hands. In any case where the same person is appointed proxy for more than one member he shall on a show of hands have as many votes as the number of members for whom he is proxy. Regulation 54 in Table A shall be modified accordingly.

4.5 Unless resolved by ordinary resolution that regulation 62 in Table A shall apply without modification, the instrument appointing a proxy and any authority under which it is executed or a copy of such authority certified notarially or in some other way approved by the directors may be deposited at the place specified in regulation 62 in Table A up to the commencement of the meeting or (in any case where a poll is taken otherwise than at the meeting) of the taking of the poll or may be handed to the chairman of the meeting prior to the commencement of the business of the meeting.

5. APPOINTMENT OF DIRECTORS

5.1.1 Regulation 64 in Table A shall not apply to the Company.

5.1.2 The maximum number and minimum number respectively of the directors may be determined from time to time by ordinary resolution. Subject to and in default of any such determination there shall be no maximum number of directors and the minimum number of directors shall be one. Whenever the minimum number of directors is one, a sole director shall have authority to exercise all the powers and discretions by Table A and by these Articles expressed to be vested in the directors generally, and regulation 89 in Table A shall be modified accordingly.

5.2 The directors shall not be required to retire by rotation and regulations 73 to 80 (inclusive) in Table A shall not apply to the Company.

5.3 No person shall be appointed a director at any general meeting unless either:-

(a) he is recommended by the directors; or

(b) not less than 14 nor more than 35 clear days before the date appointed for the general meeting, notice signed by a member qualified to vote at the general meeting has been given to the Company of the intention to propose that person for appointment, together with notice signed by that person of his willingness to be appointed.

5.4.1 Subject to Article 5.3 above, the Company may by ordinary resolution appoint any person who is willing to act to be a director, either to fill a vacancy or as an additional director.

5.4.2 The directors may appoint a person who is willing to act to be a director, either to fill a vacancy or as an additional director, provided that the appointment does not cause the number of directors to exceed any number determined in accordance with Article 5.1.2 above as the maximum number of directors and for the time being in force.

5.5 In any case where as the result of death or deaths the Company has no members and no directors the personal representatives of the last member to have died shall have the right by notice in writing to appoint a person to be a director of the Company and such appointment shall be as effective as if made by the Company in General Meeting pursuant to Article 5.4.1 above. For the purpose of this article, where two or more members die in circumstances rendering it uncertain which of them survived the other or others, the members shall be deemed to have died in order of seniority, and accordingly the younger shall be deemed to have survived the elder.

6. BORROWING POWERS

6.1 The directors may exercise all the powers of the Company to borrow money without limit as to amount and upon such terms and in such manner as they think fit, and subject (in the case of any security convertible into shares) to section 80 of the Act to grant any mortgage, charge or standard security over its undertaking, property and uncalled capital, or any part thereof, and to issue debentures, debenture stock, and other securities whether outright or as security for any debt, liability or obligation of the Company or of any third party.

7. ALTERNATE DIRECTORS

7.1 Unless otherwise determined by the Company in general meeting by ordinary resolution an alternate director shall not be entitled as such to receive any remuneration from the Company, save that he may be paid by the Company such part (if any) of the remuneration otherwise payable to his appointor as such appointor may by notice in writing to the Company from time to time direct, and the first sentence of regulation 66 in Table A shall be modified accordingly.

7.2 A director, or any such other person as is mentioned in regulation 65 in Table A, may act as an alternate director to represent more than one director, and an alternate director shall be entitled at any meeting of the directors or of any committee of the directors to one vote for every director whom he represents in addition to his own vote (if any) as a director, but he shall count as only one for the purpose of determining whether a quorum is present.

8. GRATUITIES AND PENSIONS

8.1.1 The directors may exercise the powers of the Company conferred by its Memorandum of Association in relation to the payment of pensions, gratuities and other benefits and shall be entitled to retain any benefits received by them or any of them by reason of the exercise of any such powers.

8.1.2 Regulation 87 in Table A shall not apply to the Company.

9. PROCEEDINGS OF DIRECTORS

9.1.1 A director may vote, at any meeting of the directors or of any committee of the directors, on any resolution, notwithstanding that it in any way concerns or relates to a matter in which he has, directly or indirectly, any kind of interest whatsoever, and if he shall vote on any such resolution his vote shall be counted; and in relation to any such resolution as aforesaid he shall (whether or not he shall vote on the same) be taken into account in calculating the quorum present at the meeting.

But still has to comply with CA s317

9.1.2 Each director shall comply with his obligations to disclose his interest in contracts under section 317 of the Act.

9.1.3 Regulations 94 to 97 (inclusive) in Table A shall not apply to the Company.

10. THE SEAL

10.1 If the Company has a seal it shall only be used with the authority of the directors or of a committee of directors. The directors may determine who shall sign any instrument to which the seal is affixed and unless otherwise so determined it shall be signed by a director and by the secretary or second director. The obligation under regulation 6 of Table A relating to the sealing of share certificates shall apply only if the Company has a seal. Regulation 101 in Table A shall not apply to the Company.

10.2 The Company may exercise the powers conferred by section 39 of the Act with regard to having an official seal for use abroad, and such powers shall be vested in the directors.

11. NOTICES

11.1 Without prejudice to regulations 112 to 116 (inclusive) in Table A, the Company may give notice to a member by electronic means provided that:-

11.1.1 the member has given his consent in writing to receiving notice communicated by electronic means and in such consent has set out an address to which the notice shall be sent by electronic means; and

11.1.2 the electronic means used by the Company enables the member concerned to read the text of the notice.

11.2 A notice given to a member personally or in a form permitted by Article 11.1 above shall be deemed to be given on the earlier of the day on which it is delivered personally and the day on which it was despatched by electronic means, as the case may be.

11.3 Regulation 115 in Table A shall not apply to a notice delivered personally or in a form permitted by Article 11.1 above.

11.4 In this article "electronic" means actuated by electric, magnetic, electro-magnetic, electro-chemical or electro-mechanical energy and "by electronic means" means by any manner only capable of being so actuated.

12.   INDEMNITY

12.1 Every director or other officer or auditor of the Company shall be indemnified out of the assets of the Company against all losses or liabilities which he may sustain or incur in or about the execution of the duties of his office or otherwise in relation thereto, including any liability incurred by him in defending any proceedings, whether civil or criminal, or in connection with any application under section 144 or section 727 of the Act in which relief is granted to him by the Court, and no director or other officer shall be liable for any loss, damage or misfortune which may happen to or be incurred by the Company in the execution of the duties of his office or in relation thereto. But this Article shall only have effect in so far as its provisions are not avoided by section 310 of the Act.

12.2 The directors shall have power to purchase and maintain for any director, officer or auditor of the Company insurance against any such liability as is referred to in section 310(1) of the Act.

12.3 Regulation 118 in Table A shall not apply to the Company.

13.   TRANSFER OF SHARES

13.1 The directors may, in their absolute discretion and without assigning any reason therefor, decline to register the transfer of a share, whether or not it is a fully paid share, and the first sentence of regulation 24 in Table A shall not apply to the Company.

OPTIONAL ADDITIONAL ARTICLES

(A)

●. <mark>**ENHANCED VOTING RIGHTS FOR DIRECTORS**</mark>

●.1 Every director for the time being of the Company shall have the following rights:

(a) if at any general meeting a poll is duly demanded on a resolution to remove him from office, to ten votes for each share of which he is the holder; and

change according to share.

(b) if at any general meeting a poll is duly demanded on a resolution having the effect of deleting, amending or nullifying the effect of the provisions of this Article, to ten votes for each share of which he is the holder if voting against such resolution.

●.2 Regulation 54 in Table A shall be modified accordingly.

(B)

●. **CASTING VOTE**

●. The chairman shall not, in the event of an equality of votes at any general meeting of the Company or at any meeting of the directors or of a committee of directors, have a second or casting vote. Regulation 50 in Table A shall not apply to the Company, and regulations 88 and 72 in Table A shall be modified accordingly.

(C)

●. **ASSOCIATE DIRECTORS**

●.1 The directors may at any time and from time to time appoint any employee of the Company to the position of associate director.

●.2 An associate director shall at the request of the directors advise and assist the directors but shall not attend board meetings except at the invitation of the directors, and when present at board meetings he shall not vote, nor be counted in the quorum, but subject as aforesaid he shall as associate director have such powers, authorities and duties as the directors may in the particular case from time to time determine.

●.3 An associate director shall not be deemed a member of the board, nor any committee thereof, nor shall he be a director for any of the purposes of these Articles of Association or for any of the purposes of the Act.

●.4 Without prejudice to any rights or claims the associate director may have as employee under any contract with the Company, any appointment as an associate director may be terminated by the directors at any time and shall ipso facto terminate if the associate director shall from any cause cease to be an employee of the Company.

●.5   An associate director may receive such remuneration (if any) in addition to the remuneration received as an employee of the Company as the directors shall from time to time determine.

(D)

●.   **MEETINGS**

●.1   In this Article "electronic" means actuated by electric, magnetic, electro-magnetic, electro-chemical or electro-mechanical energy and "by electronic means" means by any manner only capable of being so actuated.

●.2   A person in communication by electronic means with the chairman and with all other parties to a meeting of the directors or of a committee of the directors shall be regarded for all purposes as personally attending such a meeting provided that but only for so long as at such a meeting he has the ability to communicate interactively and simultaneously with all other parties attending the meeting including all persons attending by electronic means.

●.3   A meeting at which one or more of the directors attends by electronic means is deemed to be held at such place as the directors shall at the said meeting resolve. In the absence of a resolution as aforesaid, the meeting shall be deemed to be held at the place, if any, where a majority of the directors attending the meeting are physically present, or in default of such a majority, the place at which the chairman of the meeting is physically present.

EXPLANATORY NOTES

INTRODUCTION

The form of memorandum and articles to which these Notes are attached [Jordans M97 draft] is intended to provide a basic constitution for a private company limited by shares. Depending on the choice of location of its registered office, such a company may be incorporated in either England and Wales or in Scotland.

Whilst the specimen articles of association are primarily based on the statutory model set out in Table A of the Companies Act 1985, a number of variations have been incorporated. In particular, a number of variations and additional articles relating to other matters [optional articles (A) to (D)] have been provided. These are intended to cater for situations which our clients have found arise regularly in practice.

The attached documents have been drafted by experienced specialist Counsel as integrated documents to be read in conjunction with the relevant provisions of company law. Particular care must be taken when amending any of our standard forms. Redrafting should not be attempted without proper professional advice. **COPYRIGHT IS RESERVED IN ALL OF OUR STANDARD FORMS.**

Although the attached specimen documents are suitable for most sets of circumstance, we acknowledge that companies are incorporated for a whole host of different reasons. In particular, companies may be incorporated to pursue particular objects or to meet specific circumstances. It is not possible to anticipate all possible sets of circumstance in any standard form document. It is important for those who form companies to obtain appropriate professional advice as to whether our standard form or any of the standard variations and additional provisions are suitable for their particular requirements.

In the first instance, those wishing to incorporate a company should look to their solicitors, accountants or other appropriately qualified professional advisers for advice in such matters. Jordans are, however, able to provide bespoke drafting services to such advisers to cater for circumstances as defined by those advisers' instructions.

The obligations and responsibilities imposed on persons running limited companies are wide and far-reaching. For those unfamiliar with the responsibilities of running a private limited company, we would recommend *Running a Limited Company* (Jordans, 1996) as a valuable initial guide.

Section 3A of the Companies Act 1985 provides for a company to have a general commercial object. The object and powers set out on pages 13 to 17 are a suggested format for making use of that provision. The articles also make provision for the case where the Company may be, or become, a single member company.

For the purposes of registration, copies of the final draft must be printed for signature by subscribers and for supplying to members in accordance with section 19 of the Companies Act 1985.

COMMENTARY ON THE FORM

Notes to Memorandum

Clause 2

The country within Great Britain in which the registered office is situated must be stated – either 'England and Wales' or 'Scotland'. Alternatively, a Welsh registered office may be specified and the Welsh words 'cyfyngedig' or 'cyf' substituted for 'limited' or 'ltd' respectively in the name of the Company. The intended situation of the registered office will be set out on Form 10 filed with the Registrar of Companies as part of the incorporation procedure.

Clause 3

Section 110 of the Companies Act 1989 (which came into force on 4 February 1991) inserted a new section 3A into the Companies Act 1985. Section 3A provides that where a company's memorandum states that: 'the object of the Company is to carry on business as a general commercial company' (as set out in paragraph 3.1 on page 13) – the object of the Company is to carry on any trade or business whatsoever, and the Company has power to do all such things as are incidental or conducive to the carrying on of any trade or business by it. Section 3A draws a clear distinction between objects and powers and the proper construction of this section cannot be to exclude additional powers. Accordingly, if the wording set out in section 3A is used it would be sensible either to add the wording set out in paragraph 3.2 on page 13 followed by the wording of paragraphs 3.2.1 onwards or use other similar means to ensure that the provisions in the Company's memorandum are sufficient for its purposes.

Clause 3.1.1 – Alternative use of specific objects

Alternatively a suitable 'main objects' clause reflecting the principal business to be carried on the Company may be inserted as clause 3.1.1. This needs to be carefully and comprehensively drafted; an example is set out below, but the version used should be based on the business actually intended to be carried on. This type of main objects clause may still be used and in some circumstances will be more suitable than a general commercial company object under section 3A of the Companies Act 1985.

If an existing business or shares in an existing company are being acquired, reference to such acquisition may be desirable.

Specimen 'Main Objects' Clause

"**3.1**   The Company's objects are:

3.1.1   To create, establish and maintain an organisation for the export, import, introduction, sale, purchase, distribution, advertising or marketing of products, goods, wares and merchandise of every description; to carry on all or any of the businesses of export marketing specialists, market research advisers and consultants, mail order specialists, manufacturers' agents and representatives, importers and exporters, commission agents, general merchants and traders; and to participate in, undertake, perform and carry out all kinds of commercial, industrial trading and financial operations and enterprises; and to carry out all of the operations performed by commission and general agents, export, import and general merchants, shippers, traders, capitalists and financiers, either on the Company's own account or otherwise; and to carry on all or any of the businesses of haulage and transport contractors, garage proprietors and owners, operators, hirers and letters on hire of, and dealers in motor and other vehicles, conveyances and craft of every description, and all plant, machinery, fittings, furnishings, accessories and stores required in connection therewith or in the maintenance thereof.

3.1.2   To carry on any other trade or business whatever which can in the opinion of the board of directors be advantageously carried on in connection with or ancillary to any of the businesses of the Company."

The remaining part of clause 3 sets out additional objects which are likely to be applicable and necessary for any trading company. It is necessary for these or equivalent clauses to be set out to enable a company to carry out such objects or exercise such powers. These may be identical in format to paragraphs 3.2.1 to 3.2.23 inclusive on pages 13 to 16 but will need to be renumbered as paragraphs 3.2 to 3.24. The remainder of clause 3 might then be as follows:

"**3.24**   To do all such other things as may be deemed incidental or conducive to the attainment of the Company's objects or any of them.

3.25   AND so that:-

3.25.1   None of the objects set forth in any sub-clause of this clause shall be restrictively construed but the widest interpretation shall be given to each such object, and none of such objects shall, except where the context expressly so requires, be in any way limited or restricted by reference to or inference from any other object or objects set forth in such sub-clause, or by reference to or inference from the terms of any other sub-clause of this clause, or by reference to or inference from the name of the Company.

3.25.2   None of the sub-clauses of this clause and none of the objects therein specified shall be deemed subsidiary or ancillary to any of the objects specified in any other such sub-clause, and the Company shall have as full a power to exercise each and every one of the objects specified in each sub-clause of this clause as though each such sub-clause contained the objects of a separate company.

3.25.3   The word "company" in this Clause, except where used in reference to the Company, shall be deemed to include any partnership or other body of persons, whether incorporated or unincorporated and whether domiciled in the United Kingdom or elsewhere.

3.25.4   In this Clause the expression "the Act" means the Companies Act 1985, but so that any reference in this Clause to any provision of the Act shall be deemed to include a reference to any statutory modification or re-enactment of that provision for the time being in force."

Clause 5

Even if the share capital is to be divided into different classes of shares it is advisable (unless there is a particular requirement to entrench class rights), and usual, to omit any such division or reference to special classes in the memorandum.

Subscription

There must be shown in the memorandum against the name of each subscriber the number of shares he takes and, if the capital is divided into shares of different classes, the class subscribed for should also be stated.

The memorandum of association must be signed by at least one subscriber whose signature must be duly attested by a witness (Companies Act 1985, section 2(6)). Where there are two or more subscribers, it is permissible for one person to act as witness to them all. Underneath the signature of each subscriber and that of the witness there should be printed the full name and address of the signatory.

Notes to Articles

The first 13 articles are standard articles which are followed by special articles which can be selected and added if appropriate.

Article 1

All the regulations in Table A under the Companies Act 1985 are incorporated in these articles unless specifically stated. Where appropriate, special articles have been substituted or added.

It is convenient to bind a copy of the 1985 Table A with the articles when final prints are made. *Even if Table A changes after incorporation the Company remains subject to the version in force at its incorporation (unless it subsequently adopts new articles referring to a new Table A).*

Table A to the 1985 Act came into force on 1 July 1985 and is set out in the Companies (Tables A to F) Regulations 1985 (SI 1985 No 805). It was subject to minor amendment in the Companies (Tables A to F) (Amendment) Regulations 1985 (SI 1985 No 1052) and this final form applies as of 1 August 1985 and to these articles.

Article 2

Article 2.1 places the shares in the authorised share capital with which the Company is incorporated at the disposal of the directors to allot as they think fit. Shares subsequently created must be offered pro rata to existing members in accordance with Article 2.2. Article 2.3 excludes the statutory pre-emption rights set out in sections 89 and 90 of the Companies Act 1985. Article 2.4 gives authority under section 80 of the Act for the allotment of shares in the initial authorised share capital.

This authority is effective for five years and may be renewed. Whenever a resolution is passed creating new shares it will be normal at the same meeting to seek new authority under section 80 by ordinary resolution either in relation to that capital alone or in respect of all capital then remaining unissued. Resolutions to increase share capital and resolutions to give section 80 authority each have to be filed at the Companies Registry. The following is a possible form of resolution to give section 80 authority in respect of all unissued capital at the date of the resolution:

'That the directors be and they are hereby generally and unconditionally authorised pursuant to section 80 of the Companies Act 1985 to exercise any power of the Company to allot and grant rights to subscribe for or to convert securities into shares of the Company up to a maximum nominal amount equal to the nominal amount of the authorised but unissued share capital at the date of the passing of this resolution provided that the authority hereby given:

(a)   shall be subject to the provisions of Article 2 of the articles of association of the Company;

(b)   shall expire five years after the passing of this resolution unless previously renewed, revoked or varied save that the directors may, notwithstanding such expiry, allot any shares or grant any such rights under this authority in pursuance of an offer or agreement so to do made by the Company before the expiry of this authority.'

A different form of wording will be required if the Company has passed an elective resolution pursuant to section 80A and it is desired to give authority for an indefinite period or for a fixed period greater than five years.

Article 3.1

This article extends the Company's lien conferred by regulation 8 in Table A.

Article 3.2

This article increases the liability on defaulted calls imposed by Table A to include costs.

Article 4

Article 4.1 serves as a reminder of the statutory requirements in section 372 of the Companies Act 1985.

Article 4.2 deals with the quorum at general meetings. Article 4.2.2 is declaratory of section 370A of the Companies Act 1985 and clarifies the position of an authorised representative when a corporate body is the sole shareholder.

Article 4.2.3 alters regulation 41 in Table A so as to require a quorum to be present at an adjourned meeting and provides for the dissolution of the meeting if a quorum is not then present.

Article 4.3 contains provisions which clarify the circumstances in which and the means by which a sole member can take decisions outside a general meeting.

Article 4.4 entitles a proxy for a member to speak at a general meeting and to vote on a show of hands, contrary to the rule in Table A. Article 4.5 derogates from the inflexible rule in Table A that proxies may not be used unless lodged 48 hours before the meeting or 24 hours before the poll at which they are to be used.

Article 5

Section 13 provides that the persons named in the statement of directors filed on incorporation are to be the first directors. There is no other method of appointment.

Under Articles 5.1.1 and 5.1.2 the number of directors may be fixed by ordinary resolution of the Company. Table A is modified to provide for a sole director if required. It should be noted that a sole director may not act as secretary.

Retirement of directors by rotation is excluded. If it is desired to provide for retirement by rotation the whole of Articles 5.2 to 5.4.2 should be deleted.

Article 5.5 covers the procedure where as a result of death(s) a company has neither directors or shareholders; for example in a single member/director or husband and wife situation as a result of an accident. The last survivor in a simultaneous death is the younger person.

Article 6

Regulation 70 in Table A gives the directors authority to exercise all the powers of the company. This article is added to make it clear that they have unlimited borrowing powers and should be read in conjunction with clause 3.2.7 of the memorandum. If it is proposed to issue loan capital giving rights of conversion into share capital the issuing company should ensure that authority to allot rights to convert into shares has been given under section 80 of the Companies Act 1985.

Article 7

This article makes some practical modifications to regulations 65 and 66 of Table A in connection with alternate directors.

Article 8

The powers of the Company as to payment of pensions conferred by the memorandum are wide and extend to directors whether or not they hold or have held any executive office. This article replaces regulation 87 in Table A which limits payment of pensions to directors who have held executive office.

Article 9

Article 9.1.1 varies Table A to enable directors to vote at board meetings without restriction on matters in which they have an interest. Such provision is commonly included in the articles of private companies, but the directors (including a sole director) must still comply with section 317 of the Companies Act 1985 in disclosing interests: Article 9.1.2.

Article 10

Sections 36A and 36B of the Companies Act 1985 (as inserted by section 130 of the Companies Act 1989 and subsequent legislation) provide that a company does not have to have a common seal (although many companies may continue to have one). This article replaces regulation 101 and modifies regulation 6 in Table A so that it will be appropriate whether or not the Company has a common seal.

Article 10.2 enables the Company to have an additional seal for use abroad, in accordance with section 39 of the Companies Act 1985.

Article 11

This new article permits the Company and a member to agree that notices may be given to the member in electronic form (for example by e-mail).

Article 12

The indemnity given by this clause is wider than that provided by regulation 118 in Table A. Article 12.2 empowers directors to purchase and maintain insurance against liability of officers in accordance with the permissive power in section 310(3) of the Companies Act 1985 as altered by section 137 of the Companies Act 1989. Those wishing to take out such insurance should take advice.

Article 13

This gives the Directors absolute discretion to refuse to register a share transfer, without being required to give reasons. Restrictions on share transfers are not contained in the current version of Table A.

In many private companies the members may wish to have the right to transfer their shares to a restricted group, e.g. other members or members of their family. It may also be desired to oblige a member to make his shares available for purchase by the other members in certain circumstances, and to regulate the manner in which the price for the shares is determined. Specific transfer articles to deal with such circumstances are available if desired.

OPTIONAL ARTICLES

The following optional forms may be adopted:

A. Enhanced Voting Rights for Directors

This article reinforces the position of a director who is also a shareholder by giving such director additional votes per share on a resolution to remove him from office or amend or delete this article. Please check that 10 votes for each share is sufficient for this purpose or alter accordingly.

B. Casting Vote

This article removes the chairman's casting vote which is normally exercisable under Table A if there is an equality of votes at a general meeting or a meeting of directors. Such a provision can be useful but additional provisions may be appropriate if the articles are designed to create a 'deadlock' situation with intentionally evenly balanced representation of specific shareholding interests.

C. Associate Directors

For management purposes it may be appropriate to create a class of associate directors who are given additional status beyond that of an employee but are not members of the board. This can be useful when the appointee is in contact with customers. This additional article makes appropriate provision for a class of associate directors.

D. Electronic Attendance

This optional article enables attendance at board meetings to be by telephone or other electronic means, provided that all participants can communicate with all other parties to the meeting and that all proceedings at the meeting are communicated to him.

EXAMPLES OF

ALTERNATIVE

TRANSFER ARTICLES

USED BY JORDANS

Type 1   Optional Transfer Article

Might be used instead of Article 13 in the standard draft.

13.   TRANSFER OF SHARES

13.1   The directors shall, subject to regulation 24 in Table A, register the transfer or, as the case may be, transmission of any shares:-

13.1.1   to a member of the family of a member or deceased member;

13.1.2   to any person or persons acting in the capacity of trustee or trustees of a trust created by a member (by deed or by will) or, upon any change of trustees of a trust so created, to the new trustee or trustees (so that any such transfer as aforesaid shall be registered pursuant to this paragraph only if such shares are to be held upon the terms of the trust) provided that there are no persons beneficially interested under the trust other than the member and members of his family and the voting rights conferred by any such shares are not exercisable by or subject to the consent of any person other than the trustee or trustees of the trust or the member or members of his family and also the directors are satisfied that the trust is and is intended to remain a trust the sole purpose of which is to benefit the member or members of his family;

13.1.3   by the trustee or trustees of a trust to which Article 13.1.2 above applies to any person beneficially interested under the trust being the member or a member of his family;

13.1.4   to the legal personal representatives of a deceased member where under the provisions of his will or the laws as to intestacy the persons beneficially entitled to any such shares, whether immediately or contingently, are members of the family of the deceased member and by the legal personal representatives of a deceased member to a member or members of the family of the deceased member;

13.1.5   to any other member of the Company.

13.2   For the purpose of this Article:

13.2.1   The word "member" shall not include a person who holds shares only in the capacity of trustee, legal personal representative or trustee in bankruptcy but shall include a former member in any case where the person concerned ceased to be a member as a result of the creation of the relevant trust; and

13.2.2   the words "a member of the family of a member" shall mean the husband, wife, widow, widower, child and remoter issue (including a child by adoption), parent (including adoptive parent), brother and sister (whether of the full or half blood and including a brother or sister related by adoption), and child and remoter issue of any such brother or sister (including a child by adoption), of the member.

13.3   The directors may, in their absolute discretion and without assigning any reason therefor, decline to register any transfer or transmission of a share (whether or not it is fully paid) to which Article 13.1 above does not apply.

13.4   Regulation 24 in Table A shall be modified accordingly.

Type 2   Optional Transfer Article   See p.49 for breakdown.

Might be used instead of Article 13 in the standard draft.

13.   TRANSFER OF SHARES

13.1   Any person (hereinafter called "the proposing transferor") proposing to transfer any shares shall give notice in writing (hereinafter called "the transfer notice") to the Company that he desires to transfer the same and specifying the price per share which in his opinion constitutes the fair value thereof. The transfer notice shall constitute the Company the agent of the proposing transferor for the sale of all (but not some of) the shares comprised in the transfer notice to any member or members willing to purchase the same (hereinafter called "the purchasing member") at the price specified therein or at the fair value certified in accordance with Article 13.3 below (whichever shall be the lower). A transfer notice shall not be revocable except with the sanction of the directors.

13.2   The shares comprised in any transfer notice shall be offered to the members (other than the proposing transferor) as nearly as may be in proportion to the number of shares held by them respectively. Such offer shall be made by notice in writing (hereinafter called "the offer notice") within 7 days after the receipt by the Company of the transfer notice. The offer notice shall state the price per share specified in the transfer notice and shall limit the time in which the offer may be accepted, not being less than 21 days nor more than 42 days after the date of the offer notice, provided that if a certificate of fair value is requested under Article 13.3 below the offer shall remain open for acceptance for a period of 14 days after the date on which notice of the fair value certified in accordance with that Article shall have been given by the Company to the members or until the expiry of the period specified in the offer notice whichever is the later. For the purpose of this Article an offer shall be deemed to be accepted on the day on which the acceptance is received by the Company. The offer notice shall further invite each member to state in his reply the number of additional shares (if any) in excess of his proportion which he desires to purchase and if all the members do not accept the offer in respect of their respective proportions in full the shares not so accepted shall be used to satisfy the claims for additional shares as nearly as may be in proportion to the number of shares already held by them respectively, provided that no member shall be obliged to take more shares than he shall have applied for. If any shares shall not be capable without fractions of being offered to the members in proportion to their existing holdings, the same shall be offered to the members, or some of them, in such proportions or in such manner as may be determined by lots drawn in regard thereto, and the lots shall be drawn in such manner as the directors may think fit.

13.3   Any member may, not later than 8 days after the date of the offer notice, serve on the Company a notice in writing requesting that the auditor for the time being of the Company (or at the discretion of the auditor, a person nominated by the President for the time being of the Institute of Chartered Accountants in the country of the situation of its registered office) certify in writing the sum which in his opinion represents the fair value of the shares comprised in the transfer notice as at the date of the transfer notice and for the purpose of Article 13 reference to the auditor shall include any person so nominated. Upon receipt of such notice the Company shall instruct the auditor to certify as aforesaid and the costs of such valuation shall be apportioned among the proposing transferor and the purchasing members or borne by any one or more of them as the auditor in his absolute discretion shall decide. In certifying the fair value as aforesaid the auditor shall be considered to be acting as an expert and not as an arbitrator or arbiter and accordingly any provisions of law or statute relating to arbitration shall not apply. Upon receipt of the certificate of the auditor, the Company shall by notice in writing inform all members of the fair value of each share and of the price per share (being the lower of the price specified in the transfer notice and the fair value of each share) at which the shares comprised in the transfer notice are offered for sale. For the purpose of Article 13 the fair value of each share comprised in the transfer notice shall be its value as a rateable proportion of the total value of all the issued shares of the Company and shall not be discounted or enhanced by reference to the number of shares referred to in the transfer notice.

13.4 If purchasing members shall be found for all the shares comprised in the transfer notice within the appropriate period specified in Article 13.2 above, the Company shall not later than 7 days after the expiry of such appropriate period give notice in writing (hereinafter called "the sale notice") to the proposing transferor specifying the purchasing members and the proposing transferor shall be bound upon payment of the price due in respect of all the shares comprised in the transfer notice to transfer the shares to the purchasing members.

13.5 If in any case the proposing transferor after having become bound as aforesaid makes default in transferring any shares the Company may receive the purchase money on his behalf, and may authorise some person to execute a transfer of such shares in favour of the purchasing members. The receipt of the Company for the purchase money shall be a good discharge to the purchasing members. The Company shall pay the purchase money into a separate bank account.

13.6 If the Company shall not give a sale notice to the proposing transferor within the time specified in Article 13.4 above, he shall, during the period of 30 days next following the expiry of the time so specified, be at liberty to transfer all or any of the shares comprised in the transfer notice to any person or persons but in that event the directors may, in their absolute discretion, and without assigning any reason therefor, decline to register any such transfer and regulation 24 in Table A shall, for these purposes, be modified accordingly.

13.7 In the application of regulations 29 to 31 (inclusive) in Table A to the Company;

13.7.1 any person becoming entitled to a share in consequence of the death or bankruptcy of a member shall give a transfer notice before he elects in respect of any share to be registered himself or to execute a transfer;

13.7.2 if a person so becoming entitled shall not have given a transfer notice in respect of any share within 6 months of the death or bankruptcy, the directors may at any time thereafter upon resolution passed by them give notice requiring such person within 30 days of such notice to give a transfer notice in respect of all the shares to which he has so become entitled and for which he has not previously given a transfer notice and if he does not do so he shall at the end of such 30 days be deemed to have given a transfer notice pursuant to Article 13.1 above relating to those shares in respect of which he has still not done so;

13.7.3　　　where a transfer notice is given or deemed to be given under this Article 13.7 and no price per share is specified therein the transfer notice shall be deemed to specify the sum which shall, on the application of the directors, be certified in writing by the auditors in accordance with Article 13.3 above as the fair value thereof.

13.8　　　Whenever any member of the Company who is employed by the Company in any capacity (whether or not he is also a director) ceases to be employed by the Company otherwise than by reason of his death the directors may at any time not later than 6 months after his ceasing to be employed resolve that such member do retire, and thereupon he shall (unless he has already served a transfer notice) be deemed to have served a transfer notice pursuant to Article 13.1 above and to have specified therein the fair value to be certified in accordance with Article 13.3 above. Notice of the passing of any such resolution shall forthwith be given to the member affected thereby.

Type 3   Optional Transfer Article

Might be used instead of Article 13 in the standard draft.

13.   TRANSFER OF SHARES

13.1   The directors shall, subject to regulation 24 in Table A, register the transfer or, as the case may be, transmission of any shares:-

13.1.1   to a member of the family of a member or deceased member;

13.1.2   to any person or persons acting in the capacity of trustee or trustees of a trust created by a member (by deed or by will) or, upon any change of trustees of a trust so created, to the new trustee or trustees (so that any such transfer as aforesaid shall be registered pursuant to this paragraph only if such shares are to be held upon such terms of the trust) provided that there are no persons beneficially interested under the trust other than the member or members of his family and the voting rights conferred by any such shares are not exercisable by or subject to the consent of any person other than the trustee or trustees of the trust or the member or members of his family and also the directors are satisfied that the trust is and is intended to remain a trust the sole purpose of which is to benefit the member or members of his family;

13.1.3   by the trustee or trustees of a trust to which Article 13.1.2 above applies to any person beneficially interested under the trust being the member or a member of his family;

13.1.4   to the legal personal representatives of a deceased member where under the provisions of his will or the laws as to intestacy the persons beneficially entitled to any such shares, whether immediately or contingently, are members of the family (as hereinafter defined) of the deceased member, and by the legal personal representatives of a deceased member to a member or members of the family of the deceased member;

13.1.5   to any other member of the Company.

13.2   For the purpose of Articles 13.1 above and 13.10 below but not any other Article:

13.2.1   the word "member" shall not include a person who holds shares only in the capacity of trustee, legal personal representative or trustee in bankruptcy but shall include a former member in any case where the person concerned ceased to be a member as a result of the creation of the relevant trust; and

13.2.2   the words "a member of the family of a member" shall mean the husband, wife, widow, widower, child and remoter issue (including a child by adoption), parent (including adoptive parent), brother and sister (whether of the full or half blood and including a brother or sister related by adoption), and child and remoter issue of any such brother or sister (including a child by adoption), of the member.

13.3 Notwithstanding the provisions of Article 13, the directors may decline to register any transfer or transmission which would otherwise be permitted hereunder without assigning any reason therefor, if it is a transfer:-

13.3.1 of a share (whether or not it is fully paid) made pursuant to Article 13.9 below;

13.3.2 of a share pursuant to Article 13.1 above by a member of the Company who is employed by the Company in any capacity provided that this restriction shall not apply to such member's legal personal representatives.

Regulation 24 in Table A shall, for these purposes, be modified accordingly.

13.4 Save where a transfer is made pursuant to Article 13.1 above any person (hereinafter called "the proposing transferor") proposing to transfer any shares shall give notice in writing (hereinafter called "the transfer notice") to the Company that he desires to transfer the same and specifying the price per share which in his opinion constitutes the fair value thereof. The transfer notice shall constitute the Company the agent of the proposing transferor for the sale of all (but not some of) the shares comprised in the transfer notice to any member or members willing to purchase the same (hereinafter called "the purchasing member") at the price specified therein or at the fair value certified in accordance with Article 13.6 below (whichever shall be the lower). A transfer notice shall not be revocable except with the sanction of the directors.

13.5 The shares comprised in any transfer notice shall be offered to the members (other than the proposing transferor) as nearly as may be in proportion to the number of shares held by them respectively. Such offer shall be made by notice in writing (hereinafter called "the offer notice") within 7 days after the receipt by the Company of the transfer notice. The offer notice shall state the price per share specified in the transfer notice and shall limit the time in which the offer may be accepted, not being less than 21 days nor more than 42 days after the date of the offer notice, provided that if a certificate of valuation is requested under Article 13.6 below the offer shall remain open for acceptance for a period of 14 days after the date on which notice of the fair value certified in accordance with that Article shall have been given by the Company to the members. For the purpose of this Article an offer shall be deemed to be accepted on the day on which the acceptance is received by the Company. The offer notice shall further invite each member to state in his reply the number of additional shares (if any) in excess of his proportion which he desires to purchase and if all the members do not accept the offer in respect of their respective proportions in full the shares not so accepted shall be used to satisfy the claims for additional shares as nearly as may be in proportion to the number of shares already held by them respectively, provided that no member shall be obliged to take more shares than he shall have applied for. If any shares shall not be capable without fractions of being offered to the members in proportion to their existing holdings, the same shall be offered to the members, or some of them, in such proportions or in such manner as may be determined by lots drawn in regard thereto, and the lots shall be drawn in such manner as the directors may think fit.

13.6 Any member may, not later than 8 days after the date of the offer notice serve on the Company a notice in writing requesting that the auditor for the time being of the Company (or at the discretion of the auditor, a person nominated by the

President for the time being of the Institute of Chartered Accountants in the country of the situation of its registered office) certify in writing the sum which in his opinion represents the fair value of the shares comprised in the transfer notice as at the date of the transfer notice and for the purpose of Article 13 reference to the auditor shall include any person so nominated. Upon receipt of such notice the Company shall instruct the auditor to certify as aforesaid and the costs of such valuation shall be apportioned among the proposing transferor and the purchasing members or borne by any one or more of them as the auditor in his absolute discretion shall decide. In certifying fair value as aforesaid the auditor shall be considered to be acting as an expert and not as an arbitrator or arbiter and accordingly any provisions of law or statute relating to arbitration shall not apply. Upon receipt of the certificate of the auditor, the Company shall by notice in writing inform all members of the fair value of each share and of the price per share (being the lower of the price specified in the transfer notice and the fair value of each share) at which the shares comprised in the transfer notice are offered for sale. For the purpose of Article 13 the fair value of each share comprised in the transfer notice shall be its value as a rateable proportion of the total value of all the issued shares of the Company and shall not be discounted or enhanced by reference to the number of shares referred to in the transfer notice.

13.7 If purchasing members shall be found for all the shares comprised in the transfer notice within the appropriate period specified in Article 13.5 above, the Company shall not later than 7 days after the expiry of such appropriate period give notice in writing (hereinafter called "the sale notice") to the proposing transferor specifying the purchasing members and the proposing transferor shall be bound upon payment of the price due in respect of all the shares comprised in the transfer notice to transfer the shares to the purchasing members.

13.8 If in any case the proposing transferor after having become bound as aforesaid makes default in transferring any shares the Company may receive the purchase money on his behalf, and may authorise some person to execute a transfer of such shares in favour of the purchasing member. The receipt of the Company for the purchase money shall be a good discharge to the purchasing members. The Company shall pay the purchase money into a separate bank account.

13.9 If the Company shall not give a sale notice to the proposing transferor within the time specified in Article 13.7 above, he shall, during the period of 30 days next following the expiry of the time so specified, be at liberty subject to Article 13.3 above to transfer all or any of the shares comprised in the transfer notice to any person or persons.

13.10 In any case where any shares are held by the trustee or trustees of a trust following a transfer or transfers made pursuant to Article 13.1.2 above and it shall come to the notice of the directors that not all the persons beneficially interested under the trust are members of the family (as hereinbefore defined) of the member by whom the trust was created, the directors may at any time within 28 days thereafter resolve that such trustee or trustees do transfer such shares and such trustee or trustees shall thereupon be deemed to have served a transfer notice comprising such shares pursuant to Article 13.4 above and to have specified therein the fair value to be certified in accordance with Article 13.6 above and the provisions of Article 13 shall take effect accordingly. Notice of such resolution shall forthwith be given to such trustee or trustees.

13.11 In the application of regulations 29 to 31 (inclusive) in Table A to the Company:-

13.11.1 save where the proposed transfer or transmission is within Article 13.1 above ("a permitted transfer") any person becoming entitled to a share in consequence of the death or bankruptcy of a member shall give a transfer notice before he elects in respect of any share to be registered himself or to execute a transfer;

13.11.2 if a person so becoming entitled shall not have executed a permitted transfer or given a transfer notice in respect of any share within 6 months of the death or bankruptcy, the directors may at any time thereafter upon resolution passed by them give notice requiring such person within 30 days to execute permitted transfers or to give a transfer notice in respect of all the shares to which he has so become entitled and for which he has not previously done so and if he does not do so he shall at the end of such 30 days be deemed to have given a transfer notice pursuant to Article 13.4 above relating to those shares in respect of which he has still not executed permitted transfers or given a transfer notice;

13.11.3 where a transfer notice is given or deemed to be given under this Article 13.11 and no price per share is specified therein the transfer notice shall be deemed to specify the sum which shall, on the application of the directors, be certified in writing by the auditors in accordance with Article 13.6 above as the fair value thereof.

13.12 Whenever any member of the Company who is employed by the Company in any capacity (whether or not he is also a director) ceases to be employed by the Company otherwise than by reason of his death the directors may at any time not later than 6 months after his ceasing to be employed resolve that such member do retire, and thereupon he shall (unless he has already served a transfer notice) be deemed to have served a transfer notice pursuant to Article 13.4 above and to have specified therein the fair value to be certified in accordance with Article 13.6 above. Notice of the passing of any such resolution shall forthwith be given to the member affected thereby.

COMMENTARY ON EXAMPLES OF ALTERNATIVE TRANSFER ARTICLES

The following optional forms might be adopted instead of Article 13 in the standard draft Articles.

Type 1   Optional Transfer Article

Article 13.1 allows freedom of transfer by a member or trustees of a member's family trust to his family and in sub-paragraph 13.1.5 to other members of the company.

Transfer in these circumstances may be prevented by the directors only if the company has a lien on the share, or the share is not fully paid.

Under Article 13.3 the directors have absolute discretion as to whether or not to register any other transfer.

If unrestricted transfer between members is not required, sub-paragraph 13.1.5 of Article 13.1 should be deleted.

Type 2   Optional Transfer Article

This alternative Article sets out a full and detailed pre-emption procedure in favour of existing members: some amendment would be required for a company with more than one class of shares. A member wishing to transfer shares is required to give a transfer notice and to indicate the price which he regards as the fair value. Any would-be purchaser may request that the fair value be certified by the auditor and the auditor's 'fair value' will be adopted as the selling price if lower than the price stated by the proposing transferor (see Article 13.1). In determining the fair value of shares comprised in a transfer notice, the auditor will act as an expert and has a total discretion but is directed to fix the value of the shares as a proportion of the value of all issued shares.

Under the procedure laid down in the Article the order of events may be summarised as follows:

(1)   Any member wishing to transfer any of his shares must give a transfer notice to the company.

(2)   Not more than 7 days after receipt of the transfer notice, the company issues an 'offer notice' to its members specifying a closing date not less than 21 days and not more than 42 days after the date of the offer notice.

(3)   Within 8 days from the date of the offer notice, a would-be purchaser may ask that the Auditor certify 'fair value'. If this is requested the offer must be left open until 14 days after the company advises members of the definitive price at which the shares included in the offer notice may be purchased.

(4)   If at the close of the offer period, the company has received applications for all the shares, it must within 7 days notify the proposing transferor by a 'sale

notice' and he becomes bound upon payment of the price due to transfer the shares accordingly.

(5)   If the company has not received applications from other members for <u>all</u> the shares, the company cannot give a sale notice. If for this or any other reason the company does not give a sale notice within the due time to the proposing transferor, the proposing transferor may within a period of 30 days sell all or any of the shares included in his transfer notice to any person at any price, but the directors have an absolute right to refuse to register any such transfer.

Article 13.7 is designed to prevent shares remaining registered for long periods in the name of a deceased or bankrupt member. Six months is a suggested limit.

Article 13.8 enables the directors to deem the shares held by an employee (including a director) who has ceased to be employed to be subject to a transfer notice. This clause may be deleted if not required.

Type 3   Optional Transfer Article

This Article is in essence an amalgam of Types 1 and 2.

Article 13.10 is an additional power given to the directors to deem shares to be under a transfer notice where they become aware that there is a non-family interest in a trust. It should be deleted if not required.

Article 13.12 is optional. It is similar to Article 13.8 of Type 2. It should be noted that if an employee attempts to transfer his shares pursuant to Article 13.1, e.g. to his wife, before ceasing to be employed, sub-paragraph 13.3.2 of Article 13.3 gives the directors power to decline to register the transfer. Both sub-paragraph 13.3.2 of Article 13.3 and Article 13.12 may be deleted if not required.

The regulations of Table A to the Companies Act 1985 apply to the Company save in so far as they are excluded or varied by its Articles of Association.

Table A as prescribed by the Companies (Tables A to F) Regulations 1985 (S.I. 1985 No. 805), amended by the Companies (Tables A to F) (Amendment) Regulations 1985 (S.I. 1985 No. 1052), is reprinted below.

Table A THE COMPANIES ACT 1985

Regulations for Management of a Company Limited by Shares

INTERPRETATION

1. **In these regulations —**

'**the Act**' means the Companies Act 1985 including any statutory modification or re-enactment thereof for the time being in force.

'**the articles**' means the articles of the company.

'**clear days**' in relation to the period of a notice means that period excluding the day when the notice is given or deemed to be given and the day for which it is given or on which it is to take effect.

'**executed**' includes any mode of execution.

'**office**' means the registered office of the company.

'**the holder**' in relation to shares means the member whose name is entered in the register of members as the holder of the shares.

'**the seal**' means the common seal of the company.

'**secretary**' means the secretary of the company or any other person appointed to perform the duties of the secretary of the company, including a joint, assistant or deputy secretary.

'**the United Kingdom**' means Great Britain and Northern Ireland.

Unless the context otherwise requires, words or expressions contained in these regulations bear the same meaning as in the Act but excluding any statutory modification thereof not in force when these regulations become binding on the company.

SHARE CAPITAL

2. Subject to the provisions of the Act and without prejudice to any rights attached to any existing shares, any share may be issued with such rights or restrictions as the company may by ordinary resolution determine.

3. Subject to the provisions of the Act, shares may be issued which are to be redeemed or are to be liable to be redeemed at the option of the company or the holder on such terms and in such manner as may be provided by the articles.

4. The company may exercise the powers of paying commissions conferred by the Act. Subject to the provisions of the Act, any such commission may be satisfied by the payment of cash or by the allotment of fully or partly paid shares or partly in one way and partly in the other.

5. Except as required by law, no person shall be recognised by the company as holding any share upon any trust and (except as otherwise provided by the articles or by law) the company shall not be bound by or recognise any interest in any share except an absolute right to the entirety thereof in the holder.

SHARE CERTIFICATES

6. Every member, upon becoming the holder of any shares, shall be entitled without payment to one certificate for all the shares of each class held by him (and, upon transferring a part of his holding of shares of any class, to a certificate for the balance of such holding) or several certificates each for one or more of his shares upon payment for every certificate after the first of such reasonable sum as the directors may determine. Every certificate shall be sealed with the seal and shall specify the number, class and distinguishing numbers (if any) of the shares to which it relates and the amount or respective amounts paid up thereon. The company shall not be bound to issue more than one certificate for shares held jointly by several persons and delivery of a certificate to one joint holder shall be a sufficient delivery to all of them.

7. If a share certificate is defaced, worn-out, lost or destroyed, it may be renewed on such terms (if any) as to evidence and indemnity and payment of the expenses reasonably incurred by the company in investigating evidence as the directors may determine but otherwise free of charge, and (in the case of defacement or wearing-out) on delivery up of the old certificate.

LIEN

8. The company shall have a first and paramount lien on every share (not being a fully paid share) for all moneys (whether presently payable or not) payable at a fixed time or called in respect of that share. The directors may at any time declare any share to be wholly or in part exempt from the provisions of this regulation. The company's lien on a share shall extend to any amount payable in respect of it.

9. The company may sell in such manner as the directors determine any shares on which the company has a lien if a sum in respect of which the lien exists is presently payable and is not paid within fourteen clear days after notice has been given to the holder of the share or to the person entitled to it in consequence of the death or bankruptcy of the holder, demanding payment and stating that if the notice is not complied with the shares may be sold.

10. To give effect to a sale the directors may authorise some person to execute an instrument of transfer of the shares sold to, or in accordance with the directions of, the purchaser. The title of the transferee to the shares shall not be affected by any irregularity in or invalidity of the proceedings in reference to the sale.

11. The net proceeds of the sale, after payment of the costs, shall be applied in payment of so much of the sum for which the lien exists as is presently payable, and any residue shall (upon surrender to the company for cancellation of the certificate for the shares sold and subject to a like lien for any moneys not presently payable as existed upon the shares before the sale) be paid to the person entitled to the shares at the date of the sale.

CALLS ON SHARES AND FORFEITURE

12. Subject to the terms of allotment, the directors may make calls upon the members in respect of any moneys unpaid on their shares (whether in respect of nominal value or premium) and each member shall (subject to receiving at least fourteen clear days' notice specifying when and where payment is to be made) pay to the company as required by the notice the amount called on his shares. A call may be required to be paid by instalments. A call may, before receipt by the company of any sum due thereunder, be revoked in whole or part and payment of a call may be postponed in whole or part. A

person upon whom a call is made shall remain liable for calls made upon him notwithstanding the subsequent transfer of the shares in respect whereof the call was made.

13. A call shall be deemed to have been made at the time when the resolution of the directors authorising the call was passed.

14. The joint holders of a share shall be jointly and severally liable to pay all calls in respect thereof.

15. If a call remains unpaid after it has become due and payable the person from whom it is due and payable shall pay interest on the amount unpaid from the day it became due and payable until it is paid at the rate fixed by the terms of allotment of the share or in the notice of the call or, if no rate is fixed, at the appropriate rate (as defined by the Act) but the directors may waive payment of the interest wholly or in part.

16. An amount payable in respect of a share on allotment or at any fixed date, whether in respect of nominal value or premium or as an instalment of a call, shall be deemed to be a call and if it is not paid the provisions of the articles shall apply as if that amount had become due and payable by virtue of a call.

17. Subject to the terms of the allotment, the directors may make arrangements on the issue of shares for a difference between the holders in the amounts and times of payment of calls on their shares.

18. If a call remains unpaid after it has become due and payable the directors may give to the person from whom it is due not less than fourteen clear days' notice requiring payment of the amount unpaid together with any interest which may have accrued. The notice shall name the place where payment is to be made and shall state that if the notice is not complied with the shares in respect of which the call was made will be liable to be forfeited.

19. If the notice is not complied with any share in respect of which it was given may, before the payment required by the notice has been made, be forfeited by a resolution of the directors and the forfeiture shall include all dividends or other moneys payable in respect of the forfeited shares and not paid before the forfeiture.

20. Subject to the provisions of the Act, a forfeited share may be sold, re-allotted or otherwise disposed of on such terms and in such manner as the directors determine either to the person who was before the forfeiture the holder or to any other person and at any time before sale, re-allotment or other disposition, the forfeiture may be cancelled on such terms as the directors think fit. Where for the purposes of its disposal a forfeited share is to be transferred to any person the directors may authorise some person to execute an instrument of transfer of the share to that person.

21. A person any of whose shares have been forfeited shall cease to be a member in respect of them and shall surrender to the company for cancellation the certificate for the shares forfeited but shall remain liable to the company for all moneys which at the date of forfeiture were presently payable by him to the company in respect of those shares with interest at the rate at which interest was payable on those moneys before the forfeiture or, if no interest was so payable, at the appropriate rate (as defined in the Act) from the date of forfeiture until payment but the directors may waive payment wholly or in part or enforce payment without any allowance for the value of the shares at the time of forfeiture or for any consideration received on their disposal.

22. A statutory declaration by a director or the secretary that a share has been forfeited on a specified date shall be conclusive evidence of the facts stated in it as against all persons claiming to be entitled to the share and the declaration shall (subject to the execution of an instrument of transfer if necessary) constitute a good title to the share and the person to whom the share is disposed of shall not be bound to see to the application of the consideration, if any, nor shall his title to the share be affected by any irregularity in or invalidity of the proceedings in reference to the forfeiture or disposal of the share.

TRANSFER OF SHARES

23. The instrument of transfer of a share may be in any usual form or in any other form which the directors may approve and shall be executed by or on behalf of the transferor and, unless the share is fully paid, by or on behalf of the transferee.

24. The directors may refuse to register the transfer of a share which is not fully paid to a person of whom they do not approve and they may refuse to register the transfer of a share on which the company has a lien. They may also refuse to register a transfer unless —

(a) it is lodged at the office or at such other place as the directors may appoint and is accompanied by the certificate for the shares to which it relates and such other evidence as the directors may reasonably require to show the right of the transferor to make the transfer;

(b) it is in respect of only one class of shares; and

(c) it is in favour of not more than four transferees.

25. If the directors refuse to register a transfer of a share, they shall within two months after the date on which the transfer was lodged with the company send to the transferee notice of the refusal.

26. The registration of transfers of shares or of transfers of any class of shares may be suspended at such times and for such periods (not exceeding thirty days in any year) as the directors may determine.

27. No fee shall be charged for the registration of any instrument of transfer or other document relating to or affecting the title to any share.

28. The company shall be entitled to retain any instrument of transfer which is registered, but any instrument of transfer which the directors refuse to register shall be returned to the person lodging it when notice of the refusal is given.

TRANSMISSION OF SHARES

29. If a member dies the survivor or survivors where he was a joint holder, and his personal representatives where he was a sole holder or the only survivor of joint holders, shall be the only person recognised by the company as having any title to his interest; but nothing herein contained shall release the estate of a deceased member from any liability in respect of any share which had been jointly held by him.

30. A person becoming entitled to a share in consequence of the death or bankruptcy of a member may, upon such evidence being produced as the directors may properly require, elect either to become the holder of the share or to have some person nominated by him registered as the transferee. If he elects to become the holder he shall give notice to the company to that effect. If he elects to have another person registered he shall execute an instrument of transfer of the share to that person. All the articles relating to the transfer of shares shall apply to the notice or instrument of transfer as if it were an instrument of transfer executed by the member and the death or bankruptcy of the member had not occurred.

31. A person becoming entitled to a share in consequence of the death or bankruptcy of a member shall have the rights to which he would be entitled if he were the holder of the share, except that he shall not, before being registered as the holder of the share, be entitled in respect of it to attend or vote at any meeting of the company or at any separate meeting of the holders of any class of shares in the company.

ALTERATION OF SHARE CAPITAL

32. The company may by ordinary resolution —

(a) increase its share capital by new shares of such amount as the resolution prescribes;

(b) consolidate and divide all or any of its share capital into shares of larger amount than its existing shares;

(c) subject to the provisions of the Act, sub-divide its shares, or any of them, into shares of smaller amount and the resolution may determine that, as between the shares resulting from the sub-division, any of them may have any preference or advantage as compared with the others; and

(d) cancel shares which, at the date of the passing of the resolution, have not been taken or agreed to be taken by any person and diminish the amount of its share capital by the amount of the shares so cancelled.

33. Whenever as a result of a consolidation of shares any members would become entitled to fractions of a share, the directors may, on behalf of those members, sell the shares representing the fractions for the best price reasonably obtainable to any person (including, subject to the provisions of the Act, the company) and distribute the net proceeds of sale in due proportion among those members, and the directors may authorise some person to execute an instrument of transfer of the shares to, or in accordance with the directions of, the purchaser. The transferee shall not be bound to see to the application of the purchase money nor shall his title to the shares be affected by any irregularity in or invalidity of the proceedings in reference to the sale.

34. Subject to the provisions of the Act, the company may by special resolution reduce its share capital, any capital redemption reserve and any share premium account in any way.

PURCHASE OF OWN SHARES

35. Subject to the provisions of the Act, the company may purchase its own shares (including any redeemable shares) and, if it is a private company, make a payment in respect of the redemption or purchase of its own shares otherwise than out of distributable profits of the company or the proceeds of a fresh issue of shares:

GENERAL MEETINGS

36. All general meetings other than annual general meetings shall be called extraordinary general meetings.

37. The directors may call general meetings and, on the requisition of members pursuant to the provisions of the Act, shall forthwith proceed to convene an extraordinary general meeting for a date not later than eight weeks after receipt of the requisition. If there are not within the United Kingdom sufficient directors to call a general meeting, any director or any member of the company may call a general meeting.

NOTICE OF GENERAL MEETINGS

38. An annual general meeting and an extraordinary general meeting called for the passing of a special resolution or a resolution appointing a person as a director shall be called by at least twenty-one clear days' notice. All other extraordinary general meetings shall be called by at least fourteen clear days' notice but a general meeting may be called by shorter notice if it is so agreed:

(a) in the case of an annual general meeting, by all the members entitled to attend and vote thereat; and

(b) in the case of any other meeting by a majority in number of the members having a right to attend and vote being a majority together holding not less than ninety-five per cent in nominal value of the shares giving that right.

The notice shall specify the time and place of the meeting and the general nature of the business to be transacted and, in the case of an annual general meeting, shall specify the meeting as such.

Subject to the provisions of the articles and to any restrictions imposed on any shares, the notice shall be given to all the members, to all persons entitled to a share in consequence of the death or bankruptcy of a member and to the directors and auditors.

39. The accidental omission to give notice of a meeting to, or the non-receipt of notice of a meeting by, any person entitled to receive notice shall not invalidate the proceedings at the meeting.

PROCEEDINGS AT GENERAL MEETINGS

40. No business shall be transacted at any meeting unless a quorum is present. Two persons entitled to vote upon the business to be transacted, each being a member or a proxy for a member or a duly authorised representative of a corporation, shall be a quorum.

41. If such a quorum is not present within half an hour from the time appointed for the meeting, or if during a meeting such a quorum ceases to be present, the meeting shall stand adjourned to the same day in the next week at the same time and place or to such time and place as the directors may determine.

42. The chairman, if any, of the board of directors or in his absence some other director nominated by the directors shall preside as chairman of the meeting, but if neither the chairman nor such other director (if any) be present within fifteen minutes after the time appointed for holding the meeting and willing to act, the directors present shall elect one of their number to be chairman and, if there is only one director present and willing to act, he shall be chairman.

43. If no director is willing to act as chairman, or if no director is present within fifteen minutes after the time appointed for holding the meeting, the members present and entitled to vote shall choose one of their number to be chairman.

44. A director shall, notwithstanding that he is not a member, be entitled to attend and speak at any general meeting and at any separate meeting of the holders of any class of shares in the company.

45. The chairman may, with the consent of a meeting at which a quorum is present (and shall if so directed by the meeting), adjourn the meeting from time to time and from place to place, but no business shall be transacted at an adjourned meeting other than business which might properly have been transacted at the meeting had the adjournment not taken place. When a meeting is adjourned for fourteen days or more, at least seven clear days' notice shall be given specifying the time and place of the adjourned meeting and the general nature of the business to be transacted. Otherwise it shall not be necessary to give any such notice.

46. A resolution put to the vote of a meeting shall be decided on a show of hands unless before, or on the declaration of the result of, the show of hands a poll is duly demanded. Subject to the provisions of the Act, a poll may be demanded —

  (a) by the chairman; or
  (b) by at least two members having the right to vote at the meeting; or
  (c) by a member or members representing not less than one-tenth of the total voting rights of all the members having the right to vote at the meeting; or
  (d) by a member or members holding shares conferring a right to vote at the meeting being shares on which an aggregate sum has been paid up equal to not less than one-tenth of the total sum paid up on all the shares conferring that right;
and a demand by a person as proxy for a member shall be the same as a demand by the member.

47. Unless a poll is duly demanded a declaration by the chairman that a resolution has been carried or carried unanimously, or by a particular majority, or lost, or not carried by a particular majority and an entry to that effect in the minutes of the meeting shall be conclusive evidence of the fact without proof of the number or proportion of the votes recorded in favour of or against the resolution.

48. The demand for a poll may, before the poll is taken, be withdrawn but only with the consent of the chairman and a demand so withdrawn shall not be taken to have invalidated the result of a show of hands declared before the demand was made.

49. A poll shall be taken as the chairman directs and he may appoint scrutineers (who need not be members) and fix a time and place for declaring the result of the poll. The result of the poll shall be deemed to be the resolution of the meeting at which the poll was demanded.

50. In the case of an equality of votes, whether on a show of hands or on a poll, the chairman shall be entitled to a casting vote in addition to any other vote he may have.

51. A poll demanded on the election of a chairman or on a question of adjournment shall be taken forthwith. A poll demanded on any other question shall be taken either forthwith or at such time and place as the chairman directs not being more than thirty days after the poll is demanded. The demand for a poll shall not prevent the continuance of a meeting for the transaction of any business other than the question on which the poll was demanded. If a poll is demanded before the declaration of the result of a show of hands and the demand is duly withdrawn, the meeting shall continue as if the demand had not been made.

52. No notice need be given of a poll not taken forthwith if the time and place at which it is to be taken are announced at the meeting at which it is demanded. In any other case at least seven clear days' notice shall be given specifying the time and place at which the poll is to be taken.

53. A resolution in writing executed by or on behalf of each member who would have been entitled to vote upon it if it had been proposed at a general meeting at which he was present shall be as effectual as if it had been passed at a general meeting duly convened and held and may consist of several instruments in the like form each executed by or on behalf of one or more members.

VOTES OF MEMBERS

54. Subject to any rights or restrictions attached to any shares, on a show of hands every member who (being an individual) is present in person or (being a corporation) is present by a duly authorised representative, not being himself a member entitled to vote, shall have one vote and on a poll every member shall have one vote for every share of which he is the holder.

55. In the case of joint holders the vote of the senior who tenders a vote, whether in person or by proxy, shall be accepted to the exclusion of the votes of the other joint holders; and seniority shall be determined by the order in which the names of the holders stand in the register of members.

56. A member in respect of whom an order has been made by any court having jurisdiction (whether in the United Kingdom or elsewhere) in matters concerning mental disorder may vote, whether on a show of hands or on a poll, by his receiver, curator bonis or other person authorised in that behalf appointed by that court, and any such receiver, curator bonis or other person may, on a poll, vote by proxy. Evidence to the satisfaction of the directors of the authority of the person claiming to exercise the right to vote shall be deposited at the office, or at such other place as is specified in accordance with the articles for the deposit of instruments of proxy, not less than 48 hours before the time appointed for holding the meeting or adjourned meeting at which the right to vote is to be exercised and in default the right to vote shall not be exercisable.

57. No member shall vote at any general meeting or at any separate meeting of the holders of any class of shares in the company, either in person or by proxy, in respect of any shares held by him unless all moneys presently payable by him in respect of that share have been paid.

58. No objection shall be raised to the qualification of any voter except at the meeting or adjourned meeting at which the vote objected to is tendered, and every vote not disallowed at the meeting shall be valid. Any objection made in due time shall be referred to the chairman whose decision shall be final and conclusive.

59. On a poll votes may be given either personally or by proxy. A member may appoint

more than one proxy to attend on the same occasion.

60. An instrument appointing a proxy shall be in writing, executed by or on behalf of the appointor and shall be in the following form (or in a form as near thereto as circumstances allow or in any other form which is usual or which the directors may approve) —

'   PLC /Limited

I/We,   , of   , being a member/members of the above-named company, hereby appoint   of   , or failing him,   of   , as my/our proxy to vote in my/our name[s] and on my/our behalf at the annual/ extraordinary general meeting of the company to be held on   19 , and at any adjournment thereof.

Signed on   19   .'

61. Where it is desired to afford members an opportunity of instructing the proxy how he shall act the instrument appointing a proxy shall be in the following form (or in a form as near thereto as circumstances allow or in any other form which is usual or which the directors may approve) —

'   PLC/Limited

I/We,   , of   , being a member/members of the   above-named   company,   hereby   appoint   of   , or failing him   of   , as my/our proxy to vote in my/our name[s] and on my/our behalf at the annual/extraordinary general meeting of the company, to be held on   19 , and at any adjournment thereof.

This form is to be used in respect of the resolutions mentioned below as follows:

Resolution No. 1 *for *against

Resolution No. 2 *for *against

*Strike out whichever is not desired.

Unless otherwise instructed, the proxy may vote as he thinks fit or abstain from voting.

Signed this   day of   19 .'

62. The instrument appointing a proxy and any authority under which it is executed or a copy of such authority certified notarially or in some other way approved by the directors may —

(a) be deposited at the office or at such other place within the United Kingdom as is specified in the notice convening the meeting or in any instrument of proxy sent out by the company in relation to the meeting not less than 48 hours before the time for holding the meeting or adjourned meeting at which the person named in the instrument proposes to vote; or

(b) in the case of a poll taken more than 48 hours after it is demanded, be deposited as aforesaid after the poll has been demanded and not less than 24 hours before the time appointed for the taking of the poll; or

(c) where the poll is not taken forthwith but is taken not more than 48 hours after it was demanded, be delivered at the meeting at which the poll was demanded to the chairman or to the secretary or to any director;

and an instrument of proxy which is not deposited or delivered in a manner so permitted shall be invalid.

63. A vote given or poll demanded by proxy or by the duly authorised representative of a corporation shall be valid notwithstanding the previous determination of the authority of the person voting or demanding a poll unless notice of the determination was received by the company at the office or at such other place at which the instrument of proxy was duly deposited before the commencement of the meeting or adjourned meeting at which the vote is given or the poll demanded or (in the case of a poll taken otherwise than on the same day as the meeting or adjourned meeting) the time appointed for taking the poll.

NUMBER OF DIRECTORS

64. Unless otherwise determined by ordinary resolution, the number of directors (other than alternate directors) shall not be subject to any maximum but shall be not less than two.

ALTERNATE DIRECTORS

65. Any director (other than an alternate director) may appoint any other director, or any other person approved by resolution of the directors and willing to act, to be an alternate director and may remove from office an alternate director so appointed by him.

66. An alternate director shall be entitled to receive notice of all meetings of directors and of all meetings of committees of directors of which his appointor is a member, to attend and vote at any such meeting at which the director appointing him is not personally present, and generally to perform all the functions of his appointor as a director in his absence but shall not be entitled to receive any remuneration from the company for his services as an alternate director. But it shall not be necessary to give notice of such a meeting to an alternate director who is absent from the United Kingdom.

67. An alternate director shall cease to be an alternate director if his appointor ceases to be a director; but, if a director retires by rotation or otherwise but is reappointed or deemed to have been reappointed at the meeting at which he retires, any appointment of an alternate director made by him which was in force immediately prior to his retirement shall continue after his reappointment.

68. Any appointment or removal of an alternate director shall be by notice to the company signed by the director making or revoking the appointment or in any other manner approved by the directors.

69. Save as otherwise provided in the articles, an alternate director shall be deemed for all purposes to be a director and shall alone be responsible for his own acts and defaults and he shall not be deemed to be the agent of the director appointing him.

POWERS OF DIRECTORS

70. Subject to the provisions of the Act, the memorandum and the articles and to any directions given by special resolution, the business of the company shall be managed by the directors who may exercise all the powers of the company. No alteration of the memorandum or articles and no such direction shall invalidate any prior act of the directors which would have been valid if that alteration had not been made or that direction had not been given. The powers given by this regulation shall not be limited by any special power given to the directors by the articles and a meeting of directors at which a quorum is present may exercise all powers exercisable by the directors.

71. The directors may, by power of attorney or otherwise, appoint any person to be the agent of the company for such purposes and on such conditions as they determine, including authority for the agent to delegate all or any of his powers.

DELEGATION OF DIRECTORS' POWERS

72. The directors may delegate any of their powers to any committee consisting of one or more directors. They may also delegate to any managing director or any director holding any other executive office such of their powers as they consider desirable to be exercised by him. Any such delegation may be made subject to any conditions the directors may impose, and either collaterally with or to the exclusion of their own powers and may be revoked or altered. Subject to any such conditions, the proceedings of a committee with two or more members shall be governed by the articles regulating the proceedings of directors so far as they are capable of applying.

APPOINTMENT AND RETIREMENT OF DIRECTORS

73. At the first annual general meeting all the directors shall retire from office, and at every subsequent annual general meeting one-third of the directors who are subject to retirement by rotation or, if their number is not three or a multiple of three, the number nearest to one-third shall retire from office; but, if there is only one director who is subject to retirement by rotation, he shall retire.

74. Subject to the provisions of the Act, the directors to retire by rotation shall be those who have been longest in office since their last appointment or reappointment, but as between persons who became or were last reappointed directors on the same day those to retire shall (unless they otherwise agree among themselves) be determined by lot.

75. If the company, at the meeting at which a director retires by rotation, does not fill the vacancy the retiring director shall, if willing to act, be deemed to have been reappointed unless at the meeting it is resolved not to fill the vacancy or unless a resolution for the reappointment of the director is put to the meeting and lost.

76. No person other than a director retiring by rotation shall be appointed or reappointed a director at any general meeting unless —

(a) he is recommended by the directors; or

(b) not less than fourteen nor more than thirty-five clear days before the date appointed for the meeting, notice executed by a member qualified to vote at the meeting has been given to the company of the intention to propose that person for appointment or reappointment stating the particulars which would, if he were so appointed or reappointed, be required to be included in the company's register of directors together with notice executed by that person of his willingness to be appointed or reappointed.

77. Not less than seven nor more than twenty-eight clear days before the date appointed for holding a general meeting notice shall be given to all who are entitled to receive notice of the meeting of any person (other than a director retiring by rotation at the meeting) who is recommended by the directors for appointment or reappointment as a director at the meeting or in respect of whom notice has been duly given to the company of the intention to propose him at the meeting for appointment or reappointment as a director. The notice shall give the particulars of that person which would, if he were so appointed or re-appointed, be required to be included in the company's register of directors.

78. Subject as aforesaid, the company may by ordinary resolution appoint a person who is willing to act to be a director either to fill a vacancy or as an additional director and may also determine the rotation in which any additional directors are to retire.

79. The directors may appoint a person who is willing to act to be a director, either to fill a vacancy or as an additional director, provided that the appointment does not cause the number of directors to exceed any number fixed by or in accordance with the articles as the maximum number of directors. A director so appointed shall hold office only until the next following annual general meeting and shall not be taken into account in determining the directors who are to retire by rotation at the meeting. If not reappointed at such annual general meeting, he shall vacate office at the conclusion thereof.

80. Subject as aforesaid, a director who retires at an annual general meeting may, if willing to act, be reappointed. If he is not reappointed, he shall retain office until the meeting appoints someone in his place, or if it does not do so, until the end of the meeting.

DISQUALIFICATION AND REMOVAL OF DIRECTORS

81. The office of a director shall be vacated if—

(a) he ceases to be a director by virtue of any provision of the Act or he becomes prohibited by law from being a director; or

(b) he becomes bankrupt or makes any arrangement or composition with his creditors generally; or

(c) he is, or may be, suffering from mental disorder and either —

    (i) he is admitted to hospital in pursuance of an application for admission for treatment under the Mental Health Act 1983 or, in Scotland, an application for admission under the Mental Health (Scotland) Act 1960, or

    (ii) an order is made by a court having jurisdiction (whether in the United Kingdom or elsewhere) in matters concerning mental disorder for his detention or for the appointment of a receiver, curator bonis or other person to exercise powers with respect to his property or affairs; or

(d) he resigns his office by notice to the company; or

(e) he shall for more than six consecutive months have been absent without permission of the directors from meetings of directors held during that period and the directors resolve that his office be vacated.

REMUNERATION OF DIRECTORS

82. The directors shall be entitled to such remuneration as the company may by ordinary resolution determine and, unless the resolution provides otherwise, the remuneration shall be deemed to accrue from day to day.

DIRECTORS' EXPENSES

83. The directors may be paid all travelling, hotel, and other expenses properly incurred by them in connection with their attendance at meetings of directors or committees of directors or general meetings or separate meetings of the holders of any class of shares or of debentures of the company or otherwise in connection with the discharge of their duties.

DIRECTORS' APPOINTMENTS AND INTERESTS

84. Subject to the provisions of the Act, the directors may appoint one or more of their number to the office of managing director or to any other executive office under the company and may enter into an agreement or arrangement with any director for his employment by the company or for the provision by him of any services outside the scope of the ordinary duties of a director. Any such appointment, agreement or arrangement may be made upon such terms as the directors determine and they may remunerate any such director for his services as they think fit. Any appointment of a director to an executive office shall terminate if he ceases to be a director but without prejudice to any claim to damages for breach of the contract of service between the director and the company. A managing director and a director holding any other executive office shall not be subject to retirement by rotation.

85. Subject to the provision of the Act, and provided that he has disclosed to the directors the nature and extent of any material interest of his, a director notwithstanding his office —

    (a) may be a party to, or otherwise interested in, any transaction or arrangement with the company or in which the company is otherwise interested;

    (b) may be a director or other officer of, or employed by, or a party to any transaction or arrangement with, or otherwise interested in, any body corporate promoted by the company or in which the company is otherwise interested; and

    (c) shall not, by reason of his office, be accountable to the company for any benefit which he derives from any such office or employment or from any such transaction or arrangement or from any interest in any such body corporate and no such transaction or arrangement shall be liable to be avoided on the ground of any such interest or benefit.

86. For the purposes of regulation 85 —

    (a) a general notice given to the directors that a director is to be regarded as having an interest of the nature and extent specified in the notice in any transaction or arrangement in which a specified person or class of persons is interested shall be deemed to be a disclosure that the director has an interest in any such transaction of the nature and extent so specified; and

(b) an interest of which a director has no knowledge and of which it is unreasonable to expect him to have knowledge shall not be treated as an interest of his.

DIRECTORS' GRATUITIES AND PENSIONS

87. The directors may provide benefits, whether by the payment of gratuities or pensions or by insurance or otherwise, for any director who has held but no longer holds any executive office or employment with the company or with any body corporate which is or has been a subsidiary of the company or a predecessor in business of the company or of any such subsidiary, and for any member of his family (including a spouse and a former spouse) or any person who is or was dependent on him, and may (as well before as after he ceases to hold such office or employment) contribute to any fund and pay premiums for the purchase or provision of any such benefit.

PROCEEDINGS OF DIRECTORS

88. Subject to the provisions of the articles, the directors may regulate their proceedings as they think fit. A director may, and the secretary at the request of a director shall, call a meeting of the directors. It shall not be necessary to give notice of a meeting to a director who is absent from the United Kingdom. Questions arising at a meeting shall be decided by a majority of votes. In the case of an equality of votes, the chairman shall have a second or casting vote. A director who is also an alternate director shall be entitled in the absence of his appointor to a separate vote on behalf of his appointor in addition to his own vote.

89. The quorum for the transaction of the business of the directors may be fixed by the directors and unless so fixed at any other number shall be two. A person who holds office only as an alternate director shall, if his appointor is not present, be counted in the quorum.

90. The continuing directors or a sole continuing director may act notwithstanding any vacancies in their number, but, if the number of directors is less than the number fixed as a quorum, the continuing directors or director may act only for the purpose of filling vacancies or of calling a general meeting.

91. The directors may appoint one of their number to be the chairman of the board of directors and may at any time remove him from that office. Unless he is unwilling to do so, the director so appointed shall preside at every meeting of directors at which he is present. But if there is no director holding that office, or if the director holding it is unwilling to preside or is not present within five minutes after the time appointed for the meeting, the directors present may appoint one of their number to be chairman of the meeting.

92. All acts done by a meeting of directors, or of a committee of directors, or by a person acting as a director shall, notwithstanding that it be afterwards discovered that there was a defect in the appointment of any director or that any of them were disqualified from holding office, or had vacated office, or were not entitled to vote, be as valid as if every such person had been duly appointed and was qualified and had continued to be a director and had been entitled to vote.

93. A resolution in writing signed by all the directors entitled to receive notice of a meeting of directors or of a committee of directors shall be as valid and effectual as if it had been passed at a meeting of directors or (as the case may be) a committee of directors duly convened and held and may consist of several documents in the like form each signed by one or more directors; but a resolution signed by an alternate director need not also be signed by his appointor and, if it is signed by a director who has appointed an alternate director, it need not be signed by the alternate director in that capacity.

94. Save as otherwise provided by the articles, a director shall not vote at a meeting of directors or of a committee of directors on any resolution concerning a matter in which he has, directly or indirectly, an interest or duty which is material and which conflicts or may conflict with the interests of the company unless his interest or duty arises only because the case falls within one or more of the following paragraphs —

(a) the resolution relates to the giving to him of a guarantee, security, or indemnity in respect of money lent to, or an obligation incurred by him for the benefit of, the company or any of its subsidiaries;

(b) the resolution relates to the giving to a third party of a guarantee, security, or indemnity in respect of an obligation of the company or any of its subsidiaries for which the director has assumed responsibility in whole or part and whether alone or jointly with others under a guarantee or indemnity or by the giving of security;

(c) his interest arises by virtue of his subscribing or agreeing to subscribe for any shares, debentures or other securities of the company or any of its subsidiaries, or by virtue of his being, or intending to become, a participant in the underwriting or sub-underwriting of an offer of any such shares, debentures, or other securities by the company or any of its subsidiaries for subscription, purchase or exchange;

(d) the resolution relates in any way to a retirement benefits scheme which has been approved, or is conditional upon approval, by the Board of Inland Revenue for taxation purposes.

For the purposes of this regulation, an interest of a person who is, for any purpose of the Act (excluding any statutory modification thereof not in force when this regulation becomes binding on the company), connected with a director shall be treated as an interest of the director and, in relation to an alternate director, an interest of his appointor shall be treated as an interest of the alternate director without prejudice to any interest which the alternate director has otherwise.

95. A director shall not be counted in the quorum present at a meeting in relation to a resolution on which he is not entitled to vote.

96. The company may by ordinary resolution suspend or relax to any extent, either generally or in respect of any particular matter, any provision of the articles prohibiting a director from voting at a meeting of directors or of a committee of directors.

97. Where proposals are under consideration concerning the appointment of two or more directors to offices or employments with the company or any body corporate in which the company is interested the proposals may be divided and considered in relation to each director separately and (provided he is not for another reason precluded from voting) each of the directors concerned shall be entitled to vote and be counted in the quorum in respect of each resolution except that concerning his own appointment.

98. If a question arises at a meeting of directors or of a committee of directors as to the right of a director to vote, the question may, before the conclusion of the meeting, be referred to the chairman of the meeting and his ruling in relation to any director other than himself shall be final and conclusive.

SECRETARY

99. Subject to the provisions of the Act, the secretary shall be appointed by the directors for such term, at such remuneration and upon such conditions as they may think fit; and any secretary so appointed may be removed by them.

MINUTES

100. The directors shall cause minutes to be made in books kept for the purpose —

(a) of all appointments of officers made by the directors; and

(b) of all proceedings at meetings of the company, of the holders of any class of shares in the company, and of the directors, and of committees of directors, including the names of the directors present at each such meeting.

64

THE SEAL

101. The seal shall only be used by the authority of the directors or of a committee of directors authorised by the directors. The directors may determine who shall sign any instrument to which the seal is affixed and unless otherwise so determined it shall be signed by a director and by the secretary or by a second director.

DIVIDENDS

102. Subject to the provisions of the Act, the company may by ordinary resolution declare dividends in accordance with the respective rights of the members, but no dividend shall exceed the amount recommended by the directors.

103. Subject to the provisions of the Act, the directors may pay interim dividends if it appears to them that they are justified by the profits of the company available for distribution. If the share capital is divided into different classes, the directors may pay interim dividends on shares which confer deferred or non-preferred rights with regard to dividend as well as on shares which confer preferential rights with regard to dividend, but no interim dividend shall be paid on shares carrying deferred or non-preferred rights if, at the time of payment, any preferential dividend is in arrear. The directors may also pay at intervals settled by them any dividend payable at a fixed rate if it appears to them that the profits available for distribution justify the payment. Provided the directors act in good faith they shall not incur any liability to the holders of shares conferring preferred rights for any loss they may suffer by the lawful payment of an interim dividend on any shares having deferred or non-preferred rights.

104. Except as otherwise provided by the rights attached to shares, all dividends shall be declared and paid according to the amounts paid up on the shares on which the dividend is paid. All dividends shall be apportioned and paid proportionately to the amounts paid up on the shares during any portion or portions of the period in respect of which the dividend is paid; but, if any share is issued on terms providing that it shall rank for dividend as from a particular date, that share shall rank for dividend accordingly.

105. A general meeting declaring a dividend may, upon the recommendation of the directors, direct that it shall be satisfied wholly or partly by the distribution of assets and, where any difficulty arises in regard to the distribution, the directors may settle the same and in particular may issue fractional certificates and fix the value for distribution of any assets and may determine that cash shall be paid to any member upon the footing of the value so fixed in order to adjust the rights of members and may vest any assets in trustees.

106. Any dividend or other moneys payable in respect of a share may be paid by cheque sent by post to the registered address of the person entitled or, if two or more persons are the holders of the share or are jointly entitled to it by reason of the death or bankruptcy of the holder, to the registered address of that one of those persons who is first named in the register of members or to such person and to such address as the person or persons entitled may in writing direct. Every cheque shall be made payable to the order of the person or persons entitled or to such other person as the person or persons entitled may in writing direct and payment of the cheque shall be a good discharge to the company. Any joint holder or other person jointly entitled to a share as aforesaid may give receipts for any dividend or other moneys payable in respect of the share.

107. No dividend or other moneys payable in respect of a share shall bear interest against the company unless otherwise provided by the rights attached to the share.

108. Any dividend which has remained unclaimed for twelve years from the date when it became due for payment shall, if the directors so resolve, be forfeited and cease to remain owing by the company.

ACCOUNTS

109. No member shall (as such) have any right of inspecting any accounting records or other book or document of the company except as conferred by statute or authorised by the directors or by ordinary resolution of the company.

CAPITALISATION OF PROFITS

110. The directors may with the authority of an ordinary resolution of the company —

(a) subject as hereinafter provided, resolve to capitalise any undivided profits of the company not required for paying any preferential dividend (whether or not they are available for distribution) or any sum standing to the credit of the company's share premium account or capital redemption reserve;

(b) appropriate the sum resolved to be capitalised to the members who would have been entitled to it if it were distributed by way of dividend and in the same proportions and apply such sum on their behalf either in or towards paying up the amounts, if any, for the time being unpaid on any shares held by them respectively, or in paying up in full unissued shares or debentures of the company of a nominal amount equal to that sum, and allot the shares or debentures credited as fully paid to those members, or as they may direct, in those proportions, or partly in one way and partly in the other: but the share premium account, the capital redemption reserve, and any profits which are not available for distribution may, for the purposes of this regulation, only be applied in paying up unissued shares to be allotted to members credited as fully paid;

(c) make such provision by the issue of fractional certificates or by payment in cash or otherwise as they determine in the case of shares or debentures becoming distributable under this regulation in fractions; and

(d) authorise any person to enter on behalf of all the members concerned into an agreement with the company providing for the allotment to them respectively, credited as fully paid, of any shares or debentures to which they are entitled upon such capitalisation, any agreement made under such authority being binding on all such members.

NOTICES

111. Any notice to be given to or by any person pursuant to the articles shall be in writing except that a notice calling a meeting of the directors need not be in writing.

112. The company may give any notice to a member either personally or by sending it by post in a prepaid envelope addressed to the member at his registered address or by leaving it at that address. In the case of joint holders of a share, all notices shall be given to the joint holder whose name stands first in the register of members in respect of the joint holding and notice so given shall be sufficient notice to all the joint holders. A member whose registered address is not within the United Kingdom and who gives to the company an address within the United Kingdom at which notices may be given to him shall be entitled to have notices given to him at that address, but otherwise no such member shall be entitled to receive any notice from the company.

113. A member present, either in person or by proxy, at any meeting of the company or of the holders of any class of shares in the company shall be deemed to have received notice of the meeting and, where requisite, of the purposes for which it was called.

114. Every person who becomes entitled to a share shall be bound by any notice in respect of that share which, before his name is entered in the register of members, has been duly given to a person from whom he derives his title.

115. Proof that an envelope containing a notice was properly addressed, prepaid and posted shall be conclusive evidence that the notice was given. A notice shall be deemed to be given at the expiration of 48 hours after the envelope containing it was posted.

116. A notice may be given by the company to the persons entitled to a share in

consequence of the death or bankruptcy of a member by sending or delivering it, in any manner authorised by the articles for the giving of notice to a member, addressed to them by name, or by the title of representatives of the deceased, or trustee of the bankrupt or by any like description at the address, if any, within the United Kingdom supplied for that purpose by the persons claiming to be so entitled. Until such an address has been supplied, a notice may be given in any manner in which it might have been given if the death or bankruptcy had not occurred.

WINDING UP

117. If the company is wound up, the liquidator may, with the sanction of an extraordinary resolution of the company and any other sanction required by the Act, divide among the members in specie the whole or any part of the assets of the company and may, for that purpose, value any assets and determine how the division shall be carried out as between the members or different classes of members. The liquidator may, with the like sanction, vest the whole or any part of the assets in trustees upon such trusts for the benefit of the members as he with the like sanction determines, but no member shall be compelled to accept any assets upon which there is a liability.

INDEMNITY

118. Subject to the provisions of the Act but without prejudice to any indemnity to which a director may otherwise be entitled, every director or other officer or auditor of the company shall be indemnified out of the assets of the company against any liability incurred by him in defending any proceedings, whether civil or criminal, in which judgment is given in his favour or in which he is acquitted or in connection with any application in which relief is granted to him by the court from liability for negligence, default, breach of duty or breach of trust in relation to the affairs of the company.

Printed and supplied by

JORDANS
21 St Thomas Street Bristol BS1 6JS
Telephone: 0117 923 0600   Fax: 0117 923 0063

Please complete in typescript,
or in bold black capitals.

Notes on completion appear on final page

10

First directors and secretary and intended situation of registered office

Company Name in full

Proposed Registered Office

(PO Box numbers only, are not acceptable)

Post town

County / Region   Postcode

If the memorandum is delivered by an agent
for the subscriber(s) of the memorandum
mark the box opposite and give the agent's
name and address.

Agent's Name

Address

Post town

County / Region   Postcode

Number of continuation sheets attached

Please give the name, address,
telephone number and, if available,
a DX number and Exchange of
the person Companies House should
contact if there is any query.

Tel

DX number   DX exchange

When you have completed and signed the form please send it to the
Registrar of Companies at:
Companies House, Crown Way, Cardiff, CF4 3UZ   DX 33050 Cardiff
for companies registered in England and Wales
or
Companies House, 37 Castle Terrace, Edinburgh, EH1 2EB
for companies registered in Scotland   **DX 235 Edinburgh**

68

Company Secretary (see notes 1-5)

Company name	

NAME   *Style / Title [   ]   *Honours etc [   ]

* Voluntary details

Forename(s)	
Surname	
Previous forename(s)	
Previous surname(s)	

Address

Usual residential address
For a corporation, give the
registered or principal office
address.

Post town	

County / Region		Postcode	

Country	

I consent to act as secretary of the company named on page 1

Consent signature [   ]   **Date** [   ]

Directors (see notes 1-5)

Please list directors in alphabetical order

NAME   *Style / Title [   ]   *Honours etc [   ]

Forename(s)	
Surname	
Previous forename(s)	
Previous surname(s)	

Address

Usual residential address
For a corporation, give the
registered or principal office
address.

Post town	

County / Region		Postcode	

Country	

Day   Month   Year

Date of birth [   ][   ][   ]   **Nationality** [   ]

Business occupation [   ]

Other directorships [   ]

I consent to act as director of the company named on page 1

Consent signature [   ]   **Date** [   ]

Directors (continued)   (see notes 1-5)

	NAME	*Style / Title		*Honours etc	

* Voluntary details

Forename(s)

Surname

Previous forename(s)

Previous surname(s)

Address

Usual residential address
For a corporation, give the
registered or principal office
address.

Post town

County / Region   Postcode

Country

Day   Month   Year

Date of birth   **Nationality**

Business occupation

Other directorships

I consent to act as director of the company named on page 1

Consent signature   **Date**

This section must be signed by
Either
**an agent on behalf
of all subscribers**   Signed   Date

Or **the subscribers**   Signed   Date

**(i.e those who signed
as members on the
memorandum of
association).**   Signed   Date

Signed   Date

Signed   Date

Signed   Date

Signed   Date

Notes

1. Show for an individual the full forename(s) NOT INITIALS and surname together with any previous forename(s) or surname(s).

   If the director or secretary is a corporation or Scottish firm - show the corporate or firm name on the surname line.

   Give previous forename(s) or surname(s) except that:

   - for a married woman, the name by which she was known before marriage need not be given,

   - names not used since the age of 18 or for at least 20 years need not be given.

   A peer, or an individual known by a title, may state the title instead of or in addition to the forename(s) and surname and need not give the name by which that person was known before he or she adopted the title or succeeded to it.

   Address:

   Give the usual residential address.

   In the case of a corporation or Scottish firm give the registered or principal office.

   Subscribers:

   The form must be signed personally either by the subscriber(s) or by a person or persons authorised to sign on behalf of the subscriber(s).

2. Directors known by another description:

   - A director includes any person who occupies that position even if called by a different name, for example, governor, member of council.

3. Directors details:

   - Show for each individual director the director's date of birth, business occupation and nationality. **The date of birth must be given for every individual director.**

4. Other directorships:

   - Give the name of every company of which the person concerned is a director or has been a director at any time in the past 5 years. You may exclude a company which either **is** or at **all times during the past 5 years,** when the person was a director, **was**:

   - dormant,

   - a parent company which wholly owned the company making the return,

   - a wholly owned subsidiary of the company making the return, or

   - another wholly owned subsidiary of the same parent company.

   If there is insufficient space on the form for other directorships you may use a separate sheet of paper, which should include the company's number and the full name of the director.

5. Use Form 10 continuation sheets or photocopies of page 2 to provide details of joint secretaries or additional directors and include the company's number.

Company Secretary (see notes 1-5)

Form 10 Continuation Sheet

Company number	

NAME *Style / Title

*Honours etc

* Voluntary details

Forename(s)

Surname

Previous forename(s)

Previous surname(s)

Address

Usual residential address
For a corporation, give the registered or principal office address.

Post town

County / Region | Postcode

Country

I consent to act as secretary of the company named on page 1

Consent signature | **Date**

Directors (see notes 1-

Please list directors in alphabetical order

NAME *Style / Title

*Honours etc

Forename(s)

Surname

Previous forename(s)

Previous surname(s)

Address

Usual residential address
For a corporation, give the registered or principal office address.

Post town

County / Region | Postcode

Country

Day Month Year

Date of birth | **Nationality**

Business occupation

Other directorships

I consent to act as director of the company named on page 1

Consent signature | **Date**

72

Company Secretary (see notes 1-5)

	NAME	*Style / Title		*Honours etc	

* Voluntary details

Forename(s)

Surname

Previous forename(s)

Previous surname(s)

Address

Usual residential address
For a corporation, give the
registered or principal office
address.

Post town

County / Region		Postcode	

Country

I consent to act as secretary of the company named on page 1

Consent signature		**Date**	

Directors (see notes 1-

Please list directors in alphabetical order

	NAME	*Style / Title		*Honours etc	

Forename(s)

Surname

Previous forename(s)

Previous surname(s)

Address

Usual residential address
For a corporation, give the
registered or principal office
address.

Post town

County / Region		Postcode	

Country

	Day	Month	Year		
Date of birth				**Nationality**	

Business occupation

Other directorships

I consent to act as director of the company named on page 1

Consent signature		**Date**	

Printed and supplied by

JORDANS
21 St Thomas Street Bristol BS1 6JS
Telephone: 0117 923 0600 Fax: 0117 923 0063

12

*Please complete in typescript,
or in bold black capitals.*

Declaration on application for registration

Company Name in full

I,

of

† Please delete as appropriate.

do solemnly and sincerely declare that I am a [Solicitor engaged in the formation of the company][person named as director or secretary of the company in the statement delivered to the Registrar under section 10 of the Companies Act 1985]† and that all the requirements of the Companies Act 1985 in respect of the registration of the above company and of matters precedent and incidental to it have been complied with.

And I make this solemn Declaration conscientiously believing the same to be true and by virtue of the Statutory Declarations Act 1835.

Declarant's signature

Declared at

the   day of

One thousand nine hundred and ninety

❶ Please print name.   before me ❶

Signed   **Date**

A Commissioner for Oaths or Notary Public or Justice of the Peace or Solicitor

Please give the name, address, telephone number and, if available, a DX number and Exchange of the person Companies House should contact if there is any query.

	Tel
DX number	DX exchange

When you have completed and signed the form please send it to the Registrar of Companies at:
Companies House, Crown Way, Cardiff, CF4 3UZ   DX 33050 Cardiff
for companies registered in England and Wales
or
Companies House, 37 Castle Terrace, Edinburgh, EH1 2EB
for companies registered in Scotland   **DX 235 Edinburgh**

Printed and supplied by

JORDANS
21 St Thomas Street Bristol BS1 6JS
Telephone: 0117 923 0600   Fax: 0117 923 0063

*Please complete in typescript,
or in bold black capitals.*

30(5)(a)

Declaration on application for registration of a company exempt from the requirement to use the word "limited" or "cyfyngedig"

Company Name in full

I,

of

† Please delete as appropriate.

a [Solicitor engaged in the formation of the company][person named as director or secretary of the company in the statement delivered under section 10 of the Companies Act 1985]†do solemnly and sincerely declare that the company complies with the requirements of section 30(3) of the Companies Act 1985.

And I make this solemn Declaration conscientiously believing the same to be true and by virtue of the Statutory Declarations Act 1835.

Declarant's signature

Declared at

the _____ day of _____

One thousand nine hundred and ninety

❶ Please print name.

before me ❶

Signed _____   **Date** _____

A Commissioner for Oaths or Notary Public or Justice of the Peace or Solicitor

Please give the name, address, telephone number and, if available, a DX number and Exchange of the person Companies House should contact if there is any query.

Tel	
DX number	DX exchange

When you have completed and signed the form please send it to the Registrar of Companies at:
Companies House, Crown Way, Cardiff, CF4 3UZ   DX 33050 Cardiff
for companies registered in England and Wales
or
Companies House, 37 Castle Terrace, Edinburgh, EH1 2EB
for companies registered in Scotland   **DX 235 Edinburgh**

Printed and supplied by

JORDANS
21 St Thomas Street Bristol BS1 6JS
Telephone: 0117 923 0600 Fax: 0117 923 0063

Please complete in typescript,
or in bold black capitals.

30(5)(b)

Declaration on application for registration under section 680 of the Companies Act 1985 of a company exempt from the requirement to use the word "limited" or "cyfyngedig"

Company Name in full

I,

of

and I

of

❶ Please state whether directors or other principal officers of the company.

being ❶

do solemnly and sincerely declare that the company complies with the requirements of section 30(3) of the Companies Act 1985.
And we make this solemn Declaration conscientiously believing the same to be true and by virtue of the Statutory Declarations Act 1835.

Declarants' signatures

Declared at

the

day of

One thousand nine hundred and ninety

❷ Please print name.

before me ❷

Signed   **Date**

A Commissioner for Oaths or Notary Public or Justice of the Peace or Solicitor

Please give the name, address, telephone number and, if available, a DX number and Exchange of the person Companies House should contact if there is any query.

Tel

DX number   DX exchange

When you have completed and signed the form please send it to the Registrar of Companies at:
Companies House, Crown Way, Cardiff, CF4 3UZ   DX 33050 Cardiff
for companies registered in England and Wales
or
Companies House, 37 Castle Terrace, Edinburgh, EH1 2EB
for companies registered in Scotland   **DX 235 Edinburgh**

***Please complete in typescript,
or in bold black capitals.***

30(5)(c)

Change of name omitting "limited" or "cyfyngedig"

Company Number

Company Name in full

I,

of

❶ Please delete as appropriate.

[a director][the secretary]❶ of the company do solemnly and sincerely declare that the company complies with the requirements of section 30(3) of the Companies Act 1985.

And I make this solemn Declaration conscientiously believing the same to be true and by virtue of the Statutory Declarations Act 1835.

Declarant's signature

Declared at

the _____ day of _____

One thousand nine hundred and ninety _____

❷ Please print name.

before me ❷

Signed _____ **Date** _____

A Commissioner for Oaths or Notary Public or Justice of the Peace or Solicitor

Please give the name, address, telephone number and, if available, a DX number and Exchange of the person Companies House should contact if there is any query.

Tel

DX number   DX exchange

When you have completed and signed the form please send it to the Registrar of Companies at:

Companies House, Crown Way, Cardiff, CF4 3UZ   DX 33050 Cardiff
for companies registered in England and Wales
or
Companies House, 37 Castle Terrace, Edinburgh, EH1 2EB
for companies registered in Scotland   **DX 235 Edinburgh**

2. ADMINISTRATIVE DOCUMENTS TO BE FILED AT COMPANIES HOUSE DURING A PRIVATE LIMITED COMPANY'S LIFE

(This section is on pages 81 to 198. Contents are listed on pages 3–5)

Introduction

Notice of Accounting Reference Date (sections 224 and 225 as amended by the Companies Act 1985 (Miscellaneous Accounting Amendments) Regulations 1996 (SI 1996 No 189)).

A company's financial year for the preparation of its statutory accounts (its "accounting reference period") is determined by its accounting reference date. Its first accounting reference period commences on incorporation and ends on its accounting reference date (or seven days either side of that date, as the directors may determine). Subsequent accounting reference periods begin on the day after the end of the previous financial year and end on the accounting reference date (or seven days either side, as before).

The accounting reference date of a company incorporated on or after 1 April 1996 is automatically fixed as the last day of the month in which the anniversary of its incorporation falls. The first accounting reference period is the period of not less than six months, nor more than 18 months, beginning with its date of incorporation and ending with its accounting reference date. If the company notifies a change of accounting reference date, the first accounting reference period may be less than six months.

A company may change its accounting reference date by delivering form 225 (see page 125) to the Registrar of Companies. This may change the accounting reference date for current and subsequent accounting reference periods or, providing that it is delivered within the period allowed for delivering accounts (see below), for the immediately preceding accounting reference period. A company may not extend its accounting reference period more than once in five years (subject to certain exceptions). An accounting reference period may not in any case (unless an administration order is in force under Part II of the Insolvency Act 1986) be extended so that it exceeds 18 months.

Accounts and Reports (sections 221 to 262A)

For each accounting reference period of a company the directors of the company must prepare a balance sheet, a profit and loss account and a directors' report. Subject to exceptions, as noted below, the auditors must also make an auditors' report on the annual accounts. The accounts and reports must comply with statutory requirements. The annual accounts and directors' report must be approved by the board of directors. The balance sheet must be signed on behalf of the board by a director and the directors' report must be signed on behalf of the board by a director or secretary. The auditors' report (if required) must state the names of the auditors and be signed by them. The annual accounts and reports must be laid before the company in general meeting (unless the company has passed at the appropriate time an elective resolution to dispense with this requirement) and must also be delivered to the Registrar of Companies.

There are modified provisions regarding the content of accounts and reports for small, medium-sized and dormant companies, as set out in the Act.

Private companies which meet certain criteria do not have to have their annual accounts audited. A company is exempt from audit of the accounts for a particular financial year if:

1. it qualifies as a small company under the requirements of section 246 of the Companies Act 1985; and
2. its turnover in the year is not more than £350,000; and
3. its balance sheet total for the year is not more than £1.4 million; and
4. it is *not* during that year –
   (i) part of a group of companies; or
   (ii) a public company; or
   (iii) a banking or insurance company; or
   (iv) enrolled under section 4 of the Insurance Brokers (Registration) Act; or
   (v) an authorised person or appointed representative under the Financial Services Act 1986; or
   (vi) a special register body or employers' association as defined in sections 117 and 122 of the Trade Union and Labour Relations (Consolidation) Act 1992; or
   (vii) a charity.

A company within a group is exempt from audit of the accounts for a particular financial year if:

1. The group qualifies as a small group under the requirements of section 249 of the Companies Act 1985; and
2. The group's aggregate turnover for the year is not more than £350,000 net (£420,000 gross) (turnover calculated in accordance with section 249); and
3. The group's aggregate balance sheet total for the year is not more than £1.4 million net (£1.68 million gross) (calculated in accordance with section 249); and
4. It is *not* –
   (a) a member of an ineligible group of companies (within the meaning of section 248(2)); or
   (b) a charity.

Alternatively, a company which would otherwise be eligible for exemption but was a subsidiary undertaking in a group for all or part of the financial year is exempt from audit for that year if it was dormant for the whole of the period in that financial year whilst it was a subsidiary undertaking.

Alternatively, a company which is dormant throughout a financial year can pass a special resolution to exempt itself from audit requirements. This route is not available to banking or insurance companies or companies which are authorised persons under the Financial Services Act 1986 or obliged to prepare group accounts.

The period after the accounting reference date for laying and delivering statutory accounts is 10 months after the end of the relevant accounting reference period for a private company; seven months for a public company. These time limits are slightly modified for the accounts covering the first accounting reference period of a new company (section 244(2)). If a company has oversea interests, it can claim an extension of three months by filing form 244 – Notice of claim to extension of period allowed for laying and delivering accounts – oversea business or interests (see page 127).

Section 242A of the Companies Act 1985 provides for an automatic civil penalty which is payable to the Registrar of Companies where a company exceeds the statutory time limits referred to above for delivering its accounts and reports to Companies House. The penalty payable is in accordance with the following scale.

Length of period between latest date for delivering accounts and date of delivery	Public Company	Private Company
Not more than 3 months	£500	£100
More than 3 months but not more than 6 months	£1,000	£250
More than 6 months but not more than 12 months	£2,000	£500
More than 12 months	£5,000	£1,000

Annual Return (sections 363, 364, 364A and 365)

Every company is required to deliver to the Registrar of Companies successive annual returns, each of which is made up to a date which is not later than the company's 'return date', that is:

(a) the anniversary of the company's incorporation, *or*
(b) if the last return lodged by the company was made up to a different date, the anniversary of that date.

The annual return must be lodged within 28 days after the date to which it is made up.

Form 363a (see page 143) is prescribed for use as an annual return by the Companies (Forms) (Amendment) Regulations 1995. However, Companies House will normally issue as an annual return form 363s (the 'shuttle document' which is also a prescribed form – see page 167) to a company shortly before its 'return date'. The form 363s will contain pre-printed details of the company type, principal business activity, location of the registers of members and debenture-holders, and details of the secretary and directors. These need to be checked and the form offers the opportunity to correct or update them. Other information will be required to be inserted and usually a list of members, etc, attached.

Capital

(a) **Allotment of Shares** *(section 88)*
Notification to be given by 'Return of Allotments' on form 88(2) (Revised 1988) – Return of allotment of shares (see page 91). This form is to be filed within one month of making the allotment.

If shares are issued for a consideration OTHER THAN CASH, one of the following documents must ALSO be lodged for retention by the Registrar within one month of any allotment of shares:

(i) the contract in writing constituting allottee's title to the shares, and contract of sale; OR
(ii) if there should be no written contract, then notification must be given on form 88(3) (see page 93).

Before it will be accepted by the Registrar any such contract or form 88(3) must be duly stamped with any necessary conveyance or transfer on sale duty.

(b) **Consolidation, Sub-Division, Redemption, Cancellation, Conversion into Stock, etc** (section 122)
Notification to be given on form 122 (see page 97) within one month of such consolidation, etc.

(c) **Increase of Authorised Capital** (section 123)
Notification to be given by 'Notice of Increase' on form 123 (see page 99) within 15 days after passing of the resolution to increase capital. The resolution authorising the increase of authorised share capital must also be filed. No registration fee is charged on an increase in authorised share capital.

Registered Office (section 287(3))

A company may change its registered office by lodging form 287 (see page 129).

Directors or Secretary (sections 288, 289, 290, Schedule 1)

Notification to be given within 14 days after any change or changes in particulars of a director or company secretary on form 288a, 288b or 288c (see pages 131, 133 and 135). Form 288a is used to notify the appointment of a director or secretary, form 288b is used to notify the resignation of a director or secretary, and form 288c is used to notify any change to their particulars (eg a change of address). Persons appointed to act as a director or secretary must sign the 'consent to act' section of form 288a and all the forms must be signed on behalf of the company.

Note that not only present directorships but any directorships held within the previous five years must be included on form 288a and on the Annual Return.

Alternate directors, appointed pursuant to clauses 65 *et seq* of Table A are regarded as directors of the company in respect of whom details should be filed on the prescribed forms annotated to state that they are alternates.

Notification of interests and changes of interests in shares or debentures is to be made by the director to the company within five working days of the event (section 324, Schedule 13). Form J324/328 (which is not prescribed – see page 195 for an example) may be used for this purpose.

Notice of location of Registers etc (sections 353, 190, 325 and Schedule 13)

Notice of place where register of members is kept or of any change in that place, notice of place where a register of holders of debentures or a duplicate thereof is kept or of any change in that place and notice of place where the register of directors' interests in shares is kept or of any change in that place are to be filed at the Registry on form 353, form 190 and form 325 respectively (see pages 141, 123 and 139) and notice of place where copies of directors' service contracts or memorandum thereof are kept or of any change in that place on form 318 (see page 137). These forms need NOT be filed if the registers and documents have always been kept at the registered office of the company.

Resolutions (sections 380 and 123)

Copies of the following types of resolution must be filed within 15 days of their being passed.

Special/extraordinary (J51) (not prescribed – see page 191 for an example)
Elective (J379A) (not prescribed – see page 193 for an example)

Ordinary – *authorising increase of capital; giving, varying, revoking or renewing an authority to allot shares under section 80; revoking an elective resolution.*

Certain others agreed to by all members, OR by all members of same class of shareholders (or binding to them).

Resolution for winding up voluntarily under section 84(3) of the Insolvency Act 1986.

Registration of Particulars of Special Rights (section 128)

If a company allots shares with rights which are not stated in its memorandum or articles, or in any resolution or agreement which is required by section 380 to be sent to the Registrar of Companies, the company shall deliver to the Registrar of Companies, within one month from allotting the shares, a statement containing particulars of those rights in the prescribed Form 128(1) (see page 101).

This does not apply if the shares are in all respects uniform with shares previously allotted; and shares are not for this purpose to be treated as different from shares previously allotted by reason only that the former do not carry with the same rights to dividends as the latter during the 12 months immediately following the former's allotment.

Where the rights attached to any shares of a company are varied otherwise than by an amendment of the company's memorandum or articles or by a resolution or agreement subject to section 380, the company shall, within one month from the date on which the variation is made, deliver to the Registrar of Companies a statement containing particulars of the variation in the prescribed form 128(3) (see page 103).

Where a company (otherwise than by any such amendment, resolution or agreement as is mentioned above) assigns a name or other designation, or a new name or other designation, to any class of its shares, it shall within one month from doing so deliver to the Registrar of Companies a notice giving particulars of the name or designation so assigned in the prescribed form 128(4) (see page 105).

Memorandum and Articles of Association (sections 6 and 18)

Where a company is required to file any document making or evidencing an alteration in its memorandum or articles of association (other than a special resolution making alterations to its objects under section 4) the company MUST SEND with it a PRINTED COPY OF THE MEMORANDUM OR ARTICLES AS ALTERED (section 18).

Where a resolution altering a company's objects is passed, a PRINTED COPY OF THE MEMORANDUM AS ALTERED must still be filed, but different time limits apply (section 6).

Removal and Resignation of Auditors (sections 391 to 394A as substituted by sections 122 and 123 of the Companies Act 1989)

Notice of passing of resolution removing an auditor under section 391 is to be filed within 14 days on form 391 (see page 173).

Where an auditor ceases for any reason to hold office, he must (in accordance with time limits set out in the Act) deposit a statement at the company's registered office of any circumstances connected with his ceasing to hold office which he considers should be brought to the attention of the members or creditors of the company or, if he considers that there are no such circumstances, a statement that there are none. In the former case, unless the auditor receives notice within 21 days that the company is making an application to the court regarding the statement, *the auditor* must, within a further seven days, send a copy of the statement to the Registrar of Companies. Form J394 (which is not prescribed – see page 197 for an example) may be used for this purpose.

Charges, Mortgages and Debentures (section 395 *et seq*)

Notification of particulars of most mortgages or charges created by a company must be given to the Registrar within 21 days after the date of their creation and the relative instrument (if any) creating the charge MUST ALSO BE PRODUCED at the same time. The appropriate form will, in many cases, be form 395 (see page 175) (form 410 in Scotland) and must be fully completed.

The following other forms are used in the specific circumstances of:

Particulars for the registration of a charge to secure a series of debentures	Form 397 (see page 177) (Form 413 in Scotland)
Particulars of a mortgage or charge subject to which property has been acquired	Form 400 (see page 181) (Form 416 in Scotland)
Particulars of an issue of secured debentures in a series	Form 397(a) (see page 179) (Form 413a in Scotland)

When a charge has been wholly or partially redeemed a DECLARATION OF SATISFACTION may be lodged with the Registrar, using form 403a (see page 183) (form 419a in Scotland).

Alternatively, where the declaration relates to:

(1) release of part of property or undertaking from the charge

(2) or where that part of the property or undertaking charged no longer forms part of the company's property or undertaking

a completed form 403b (see page 185) (form 419b in Scotland) should be so lodged.

Re-registration of a Private Company as a Public Company

The Companies Act 1985 specifically defines a public company (section 1) which is required to be registered as such and sections 43, 44, 46 and 47 provide for the re-registration of a private company as a public company.

Application for re-registration is made on form 43(3) (see page 87) supported by a statutory declaration on form 43(3)(e) (see page 89) and the other documents listed in form 43(3) together with special resolution(s) to re-register and make any required alterations to the memorandum and articles of association.

Financial Assistance for Acquisition of Shares (sections 151 *et seq*)

Although the giving of financial assistance by a company for acquisition of shares in itself or its holding company is generally prohibited, certain categories of assistance are specified as permissible within the terms of these sections. Forms 155(6)a, 155(6)b and 157 have been prescribed in relation to them (see pages 107, 111 and 115).

Purchase and Redemption by Private Company of Own Shares (sections 159–78)

Forms 169, 173 and 176, which have been prescribed in relation to certain of these sections, are shown (see pages 117, 119 and 121).

Voluntary Striking Off (sections 652A to 652F inserted by the Deregulation and Contracting Out Act 1994)

Forms 652a and 652c have been prescribed for making an application for the voluntary striking off of a company and for the withdrawal of such an application (see pages 187 and 189). Detailed requirements apply in connection with making such application.

The above notes are not exhaustive, but they are likely to cover the principal formalities to be observed by a private limited company.

Printed and supplied by

JORDANS
21 St Thomas Street Bristol BS1 6JS
Telephone: 0117 923 0600   Fax: 0117 923 0063

Please complete in typescript,
or in bold black capitals.

43(3)

Application by a private company for re-registration as a public company

Company Number [   ]

Company Name in full [   ]

applies to be re-registered as a public company by the name of:

❶ [   ]

and for that purpose delivers the following documents for registration:

❶ Please insert full name of company amended to make it appropriate for this company as a public limited company.

1. A declaration on form 43(3)(e) by a director or secretary, according to section 43(3)(e) of the Companies Act 1985

2. A printed copy of the memorandum and articles as altered in pursuance of the special resolution under section 43(1)(a) of the above Act

3. A copy of the auditors written statement in relation to section 43(3)(b) of the above Act

4. A copy of the relevant balance sheet with the auditors unqualified report

❷ Please delete if section 44 of the Act does not apply.

❷ 5. A copy of any valuation report.

Signed [   ] **Date** [   ]

† Please delete as appropriate.

Please give the name, address, telephone number and, if available, a DX number and Exchange of the person Companies House should contact if there is any query.

† a director / secretary

[   ]

Tel

DX number   DX exchange

When you have completed and signed the form please send it to the Registrar of Companies at:
Companies House, Crown Way, Cardiff, CF4 3UZ   DX 33050 Cardiff
for companies registered in England and Wales
or
Companies House, 37 Castle Terrace, Edinburgh, EH1 2EB
for companies registered in Scotland   **DX 235 Edinburgh**

*Please complete in typescript,
or in bold black capitals.*

43(3)(e)

**Declaration on application by a private company for
re-registration as a public company**

Company Number

Company Name in full

I,

of

❶ Please delete
as appropriate.

❶ [a director][the secretary] of the company do solemnly and sincerely declare that:

Day   Month   Year

1. the company passed a special resolution on   that the company be
   re-registered as a public company;
2. the conditions of sections 44 and 45 of the Companies Act 1985 (so far as applicable) have been satisfied;
3. between the balance sheet date and the application for re-registration, there has been no change
   in the company's financial position resulting in the amount of its net assets becoming less than the
   sum of its called-up share capital and undistributable reserves.

And I make this solemn Declaration conscientiously believing the same to be true and by virtue of the
Statutory Declarations Act 1835

Declarant's signature

Declared at

the   day of

One thousand nine hundred and ninety

❷ Please print name.

before me **❷**

Signed   **Date**

A Commissioner for Oaths or Notary Public or Justice of the Peace or Solicitor

Please give the name, address,
telephone number and, if available,
a DX number and Exchange of
the person Companies House should
contact if there is any query.

Tel

DX number   DX exchange

When you have completed and signed the form please send it to the
Registrar of Companies at:
Companies House, Crown Way, Cardiff, CF4 3UZ   DX 33050 Cardiff
for companies registered in England and Wales
or
Companies House, 37 Castle Terrace, Edinburgh, EH1 2EB
for companies registered in Scotland   **DX 235 Edinburgh**

G

COMPANIES FORM No. 88(2)(Rev 1988)

Return of allotments of shares

Pursuant to section 88(2) of the Companies Act 1985 (the Act)

88(2)

(REVISED 1988)

This form replaces forms
PUC2, PUC3 and 88(2)

Please do not
write in this
margin

To the Registrar of Companies (**address overleaf**)
(see note 1)

**Please complete
legibly, preferably
in black type, or
bold block lettering**

Company Number

1. Name of company

* insert full name
of company

*

2. This section must be completed for all allotments

* distinguish
between
ordinary
preference, etc

Descriptions of shares†			
A Number allotted			
B Nominal value of each	£	£	£
C Total amount (if any) paid or due and payable on each share (including premium if any)	£	£	£

§ complete
(a) or (b) as
appropriate

Date(s) on which the shares were allotted

(a) [on_____ 19_____]§, or

(b) [from_____ 19_____ to _____ 19_____]§

The names and addresses of the allottees and the number of shares allotted to each should be given overleaf

3. If the allotment is wholly or partly other than for cash the following information must be given **(see notes 2 & 3)**

D Extent to which each share is to be treated as paid up. Please use percentage.			
E Consideration for which the shares were allotted _____			

NOTES

1. This form should be delivered to the Registrar of Companies within one month of the (first) date of allotment.

2. If the allotment is wholly or partly other than for cash, the company must deliver to the registrar a return containing the information at D & E. The company may deliver this information by completing D & E and the delivery of the information must be accompanied by the duly stamped contract required by section 88(2)(b) of the Act or by the duly stamped prescribed particulars required by section 88(3) (Form No 88(3)).

3. Details of bonus issues should be included only in section 2.

Presentor's name address, telephone
number and reference (if any):

For official Use	Post Room

Page 1

JORDANS

92

4. Names and addresses of the allottees

Names and Addresses	Number of shares allotted		
	Ordinary	Preference	Other
Total			

Where the space given on this form is inadequate, continuation sheets should be used and the number of sheets attached should be indicated in the box opposite:

‡ Insert, Director, Secretary, Administrator, Administrative Receiver or Receiver (Scotland) as appropriate.

Signed _____ Designation‡ _____ Date_____

Companies registered in England and Wales or Wales should deliver this form to:-

The Registrar of Companies
Companies House
Crown Way
Maindy
Cardiff
CF4 3UZ

Companies registered in Scotland should deliver this form to:-

The Registrar of Companies
Companies Registration Office
102 George Street
Edinburgh
EH2 3DJ

2.89

G

COMPANIES FORM No. 88(3)

Particulars of a contract relating to shares allotted as fully or partly paid up otherwise than in cash

Pursuant to section 88(3) of the Companies Act 1985

Note: This form is only for use when the contract has not been reduced to writing

Please complete legibly, preferably in black type, or bold block lettering

To the Registrar of Companies

For official use

Company number

Please do not write in the space below. For Inland Revenue use only

The particulars must be stamped with the same stamp duty as would have been payable if the contract had been reduced to writing. A reduced rate of ad valorem duty may be available if this form is properly certified at the appropriate amount.

Name of company

* insert full name of company

*

gives the following particulars of a contract which has not been reduced to writing

1 The number of shares allotted as fully or partly paid up otherwise than in cash

2 The nominal value of each such share   £ ,

3a The amount of such nominal value to be considered as paid up on each share otherwise than in cash   £

b The value of each share allotted i.e. the nominal value and any premium   £

c The amount to be considered as paid up in respect of b   £

4 If the consideration for the allotment of such shares is services, or any consideration other than that mentioned below in 8, state the nature and amount of such consideration, and the number of shares allotted

Presentor's name address and reference (if any):

For official Use

Capital Section

Post room

Page 1

JORDANS

94

5 If the allotment is a bonus issue, state the amount of reserves capitalised in respect of this issue

£

6 If the allotment is made in consideration of the release of a debt, e.g., a director's loan account, state the amount released

£

7 If the allotment is made in connection with the conversion of loan stock, state the amount of stock converted in respect of this issue

£

8 If the allotment is made in satisfaction or part satisfaction of the purchase price of property, give below:

a brief description of property:

b *full particulars of the manner in which the purchase price is to be satisfied*

£   p

Amount of consideration payable in cash or bills ....

Amount of consideration payable in debentures, etc......

Amount of consideration payable in shares ....

Liabilities of the vendor assumed by the purchaser:

Amounts due on mortgages of freeholds and/or

leaseholds including interest to date of sale ....

Hire purchase etc debts in respect of goods acquired ...

Other liabilities of the vendor,..

Any other consideration ....

9 Give full particulars in the form of the following table, of the property which is the subject of the sale, showing in detail how the total purchase price is apportioned between the respective heads:

	£
Legal estates in freehold property and fixed plant and machinery and other fixtures thereon*	
Legal estates in leasehold property*	
Fixed plant and machinery on leasehold property (including tenants', trade and other fixtures)	
Equitable interests in freehold or leasehold property*	
Loose plant and machinery, stock-in-trade and other chattels (plant and machinery should not be included under this head unless it was in actual state of severance on the date of the sale)	
Goods, wares and merchandise subject to hire purchase or other agreements (written down value)	
Goodwill and benefit of contracts	
Patents, designs, trademarks, licences, copyrights, etc.	
Book and other debts	
Cash in hand and at bank on current account, bills, notes, etc	
Cash on deposit at bank or elsewhere	
Shares, debentures and other investments	
Other property	

Signed   Designation‡   Date

Certificate of value§

It is certified that the transaction effected by the contract does not form part of a larger transaction or series of transactions in respect of which the amount or value, or aggregate amount or value, of the consideration exceeds £

Signed   Date

Signed   Date

G

COMPANIES FORM No. 122

Notice of consolidation, division, sub-division, redemption or cancellation of shares, or conversion, re-conversion of stock into shares

122

Pursuant to section 122 of the Companies Act 1985

Please do not write in this margin

Please complete legibly, preferably in black type, or bold block lettering

To the Registrar of Companies

For official use

Company number

Name of company

* insert full name of company

*

gives notice that:

‡ Insert Director, Secretary, Administrator, Administrative Receiver or Receiver (Scotland) as appropriate

Signed   Designation‡   Date

Presentor's name address and reference (if any):

For official Use

General Section   Post room

JORDANS

G

COMPANIES FORM No. 123

Notice of increase
in nominal capital

123

Please do not
write in
this margin

Pursuant to section 123 of the Companies Act 1985

**Please complete
legibly, preferably
in black type, or
bold block lettering**

To the Registrar of Companies

For official use   Company number

⌐ ¬ ¬ ¬ ¬
ı ı ı ı
∟ ┘ ┘ ┘

Name of company

* insert full name
of company

*

gives notice in accordance with section 123 of the above Act that by resolution of the company

dated _____the nominal capital of the company has been

increased by £ _____ beyond the registered capital of £ _____.

§ the copy must be
printed or in some
other form approved
by the registrar

A copy of the resolution authorising the increase is attached.§

The conditions (eg. voting rights, dividend rights, winding-up rights etc.) subject to which the new

shares have been or are to be issued are as follow:

‡ Insert
Director,
Secretary,
Administrator,
Administrative
Receiver or
Receiver
(Scotland) as
appropriate

Please tick here if
continued overleaf

Signed   Designation‡   Date

Presentor's name address and
reference (if any):

For official Use

General Section | Post room

JORDANS

Supplied by Jordans Limited   Tel. 0117 923 0600

G

COMPANIES FORM No. 128(1)

Statement of rights
attached to allotted shares

Pursuant to section 128(1) of the Companies Act 1985

Please do not
write in
this margin

**Please complete
legibly, preferably
in black type, or
bold block lettering**

To the Registrar of Companies

For official use

Company number

* insert full
name of
company

Name of company

*

has allotted shares with rights which:

    i. are not stated in the company's memorandum or articles or in any resolution or agreement to

    which section 380 of the above Act applies, and

    ii. are not in all respects uniform with those attached to shares previously allotted.

† delete as
appropriate

The class[es]† of such shares and the date of the first allotment of shares in each class and the rights

attached to each class are:

Class of Shares	Date of first allotment
Description of Rights	

‡ Insert
Director,
Secretary,
Administrator,
Administrative
Receiver or
Receiver
(Scotland) as
appropriate

Signed   Designation‡   Date

Presentor's name address and
reference (if any):

For official Use

General Section   Post room

JJ
J O R D A N S

Supplied by Jordans Limited   Tel. 0117 923 0600

COMPANIES FORM No. 128(3)

Statement of particulars of variation of rights attached to shares

128(3)

Pursuant to section 128(3) of the Companies Act 1985

Please complete legibly, preferably in black type, or bold block lettering

* insert full name of company

§ insert date

For official use

Company number

Name of company

*

On § _____ the rights attached to

Number of Shares	Class(es) of share

were varied as set out below (otherwise than by amendment of the company's memorandum or

articles or by any resolution or agreement to which section 380 of the above Act applies)

‡ Insert Director, Secretary, Administrator, Administrative Receiver or Receiver (Scotland) as appropriate

Signed   Designation‡   Date

Presentor's name address and reference (if any):

For official Use

General Section   Post room

JORDANS

Supplied by Jordans Limited   Tel. 0117 923 0600

105

G

COMPANIES FORM No. 128(4)

Notice of assignment of name or new name to any class of shares

128(4)

Pursuant to section 128(4) of the Companies Act 1985

Please do not write in this margin

Please complete legibly, preferably in black type, or bold block lettering

* insert full name of company

† delete as appropriate

To the Registrar of Companies

For official use

Company number

Name of company

*

gives notice of the assignment of a [new]† name or other designation to the following class[es]† of shares (otherwise than by amendment of the company's memorandum or articles or by any resolution or agreement to which section 380 of the above Act applies)

Number and class of shares	Name or other designation

‡ Insert Director, Secretary, Administrator, Administrative Receiver or Receiver (Scotland) as appropriate

Signed   Designation‡   Date

Presentor's name address and reference (if any):

For official Use

General Section   Post room

JORDANS

Supplied by Jordans Limited   Tel. 0117 923 0600

COMPANIES FORM No.155(6)a

Declaration in relation to assistance for the acquisition of shares.

Pursuant to section 155(6) of the Companies Act 1985

Please do not write in this margin

Please complete legibly, preferably in black type, or bold block lettering

Note
Please read the notes on page 3 before completing this form.

* insert full name of company

ø insert name(s) and address(es) of all the directors

To the Registrar of Companies

For official use

Company number

Name of company

*

I/We ø _____

_____

_____

_____

_____

_____

_____

_____

† delete as appropriate

[the sole director][all the directors]† of the above company do solemnly and sincerely declare that:

The business of the company is:

(a) that of a [recognised bank][licensed institution]† within the meaning of the Banking Act 1979§

§ delete whichever is inappropriate

(b) that of a person authorised under section 3 or 4 of the Insurance Companies Act 1982 to carry on insurance business in the United Kingdom§

(c) something other than the above§

The company is proposing to give financial assistance in connection with the acquisition of shares in the [company] [company's holding company _____

_____ Limited]†

The assistance is for the purpose of [that acquisition][reducing or discharging a liability incurred for the purpose of that acquisition].†

The number and class of the shares acquired or to be acquired is: _____

_____

Presentor's name address and reference (if any):

For official Use

General Section

Post room

Page 1

JORDANS

Supplied by Jordans Limited   Tel. 0117 923 0600

108

The assistance is to be given to: (note 2) _____

_____

_____

_____

**Please complete
legibly, preferably
in black type, or
bold block lettering**

The assistance will take the form of:

```
┌──────────────────────────────────────────────────┐
│                                                    │
│                                                    │
│                                                    │
│                                                    │
│                                                    │
│                                                    │
│                                                    │
│                                                    │
│                                                    │
│                                                    │
└──────────────────────────────────────────────────┘
```

The person who [has acquired][will acquire]† the shares is:

† delete as
   appropriate

_____

_____

The principal terms on which the assistance will be given are:

```
┌──────────────────────────────────────────────────┐
│                                                    │
│                                                    │
│                                                    │
│                                                    │
│                                                    │
│                                                    │
│                                                    │
│                                                    │
│                                                    │
└──────────────────────────────────────────────────┘
```

The amount of cash to be transferred to the person assisted is £_____

The value of any asset to be transferred to the person assisted is £_____

The date on which the assistance is to be given is _____ 19 _____

Page 2

**Please complete
legibly, preferably
in black type, or
bold block lettering**

I/We have formed the opinion, as regards the company's initial situation immediately following the date on which the assistance is proposed to be given, that there will be no ground on which it could then be found to be unable to pay its debts.(note 3)

* delete either (a) or
(b) as appropriate

(a)[I/We have formed the opinion that the company will be able to pay it's debts as they fall due during the year immediately following that date]*(note 3)

(b)[It is intended to commence the winding-up of the company within 12 months of that date, and I/we have formed the opinion that the company will be able to pay its debts in full within 12 months of the commencement of the winding up.]*(note 3)

And I/we make this solemn declaration conscientiously believing the same to be true and by virtue of the provisions of the Statutory Declarations Act 1835.

Declared at _____

_____

_____

the _____ day of _____

one thousand nine hundred and _____

_____

before me _____

A Comissioner for Oaths or Notary Public or Justice of
the Peace or a Solicitor having the powers conferred on
a Comissioner for Oaths.

Declarants to sign below

NOTES

1   For the meaning of "a person incurring a liability" and "reducing or discharging a liability" see section 152(3) of the Companies Act 1985.

2   Insert full name(s) and address(es) of the person(s) to whom assistance is to be given; if a recipient is a company the registered office address should be shown.

3   Contingent and prospective liabilities of the company are to be taken into account - see section 156(3) of the Companies Act 1985.

4   The auditors report required by section 156(4) of the Companies Act 1985 must be annexed to this form.

G

COMPANIES FORM No. 155(6)b

Declaration by the directors of a holding company in relation to assistance for the acquisition of shares

Please do not write in this margin

Pursuant to section 155(6) of the Companies Act 1985

Please complete legibly, preferably in black type, or bold block lettering

To the Registrar of Companies   For official use   Company number

Name of company

Note
Please read the notes on page 3 before completing this form.

*

* insert full name of company

I/We ø _____

ø insert name(s) and address(es) of all the directors

_____

_____

_____

_____

_____

_____

_____

† delete as appropriate

[the sole director][all the directors]† of the above company (hereinafter called 'this company') do solemnly and sincerely declare that:

§ delete whichever is inappropriate

The business of this company is:

(a) that of a [recognised bank][licensed institution]† within the meaning of the Banking Act 1979§

(b) that of a person authorised under section 3 or 4 of the Insurance Companies Act 1982 to carry on insurance business in the United Kingdom§

(c) something other than the above§

This company is [the][a] holding company of* _____

_____ which is

proposing to give financial assistance in connection with the acquisition of shares

in [this company][_____

_____ the holding company of this company.]†

Presentor's name address and reference (if any):

For official Use	
General Section	Post room

Page 1

JORDANS

Supplied by Jordans Limited   Tel. 0117 923 0600

112

The assistance is for the purpose of [that acquisition][reducing or discharging a liability incurred for the purpose of that acquisition].† (note 1)

The number and class of the shares acquired or to be acquired is: _____ _____

The assistance is to be given to: (note 2) _____ _____ _____ _____

The assistance will take the form of:

```



```

The person who [has acquired][will acquire]† the shares is: _____ _____

The principal terms on which the assistance will be given are:

```



```

The amount (if any) by which the net assets of the company which is giving the assistance will be reduced by giving it is _____

The amount of cash to be transferred to the person assisted is £_____

The value of any asset to be transferred to the person assisted is £_____

Page 2

The date on which the assistance is to be given is_____ 19 _____

I/We have formed the opinion, as regards this company's initial situation immediately following the date on which the assistance is proposed to be given, that there will be no ground on which it could then be found to be unable to pay its debts.(note 3)

(a)[I/We have formed the opinion that this company will be able to pay it's debts as they fall due during the year immediately following that date]*(note 3)

(b)[It is intended to commence the winding-up of this company within 12 months of that date, and I/we have formed the opinion that this company will be able to pay its debts in full within 12 months of the commencement of the winding up.]*(note 3)

And I/we make this solemn declaration conscientiously believing the same to be true and by virtue of the provisions of the Statutory Declarations Act 1835.

Declared at _____   Declarants to sign below

_____

_____

the_____ day of _____

one thousand nine hundred and _____

_____

before me _____

A Commissioner for Oaths or Notary Public or Justice of
the Peace or a Solicitor having the powers conferred on a
Commissioner for Oaths.

NOTES

1   For the meaning of "a person incurring a liability" and "reducing or discharging a liability" see section 152(3) of the Companies Act 1985.

2   Insert full name(s) and address(es) of the person(s) to whom assistance is to be given; if a recipient is a company the registered office address should be shown.

3   Contingent and prospective liabilities of the company are to be taken into account - see section 156(3) of the Companies Act 1985.

4   The auditors report required by section 156(4) of the Companies Act 1985 must be annexed to this form.

G

COMPANIES FORM No. 157

Notice of application made to the Court for the cancellation of a special resolution regarding financial assistance for the acquisition of shares

Pursuant to section 157(3) of the Companies Act 1985

Please complete legibly, preferably in black type, or bold block lettering

To the Registrar of Companies

For official use

Company number

* insert full name
of company

Name of company

*

gives notice that an application has been made to the Court on _____

for the cancellation of the special resolution passed by the company on _____

approving the giving of financial assistance by

† delete as
appropriate

    [the company]†

ø insert full name of the
subsidiary company
proposing to give
the financial
assistance

    [the company's subsidiary ø _____

    _____]†

for the purchase of shares :—

    (a) [in the company]†

§ insert full name
of the holding
company in
relation to the
acquisition of
whose shares
financial assistance
is proposed to be
given

    (b) [in § _____

_____ , the company's holding company].†

‡ Insert
Director,
Secretary,
Administrator,
Administrative
Receiver or
Receiver
(Scotland) as
appropriate

Signed   Designation‡   Date

Presentor's name address and
reference (if any):

For official Use

General Section   Post room

JORDANS

Supplied by Jordans Limited   Tel. 0117 923 0600

G

COMPANIES FORM No. 169

Return by a company purchasing its own shares

169

Pursuant to section 169 of the Companies Act 1985

Please do not
write in
this margin

To the Registrar of Companies

Please do not write
in the space below.
For Inland Revenue
use only.

**Please complete
legibly, preferably
in black type, or
bold block lettering**

	For official use	Company number

Name of company

* insert full name
of company

*

Note
This return must be
delivered to the
Registrar within a
period of 28 days
beginning with the
first date on which
shares to which it
relates were delivered
to the company

Shares were purchased by the company under section 162 of the above Act as follows:

Class of shares			
Number of shares purchased			
Nominal value of each share			
Date(s) on which the shares were delivered to the company			
Maximum prices paid § for each share			
Minimum prices paid § for each share			

§ A private company
is not required to
give this information

The aggregate amount paid by the company for the shares to which this return relates was:	£
Stamp duty payable pursuant to section 66 of the Finance Act 1986 on the aggregate amount at 50p per £100 or part of £100	£

‡ Insert
Director,
Secretary,
Receiver,
Administrator,
Administrative
Receiver or
Receiver
(Scotland) as
appropriate

Signed   Designation‡   Date

Presenter's name address and
reference (if any):

For official Use	
General Section	Post room

JORDANS

Supplied by Jordans Limited   Tel. 0117 923 0600

G

COMPANIES FORM No.173

Declaration in relation to the redemption or purchase of shares out of capital

173

Pursuant to section 173 of the Companies Act 1985

Please do not
write in
this margin

**Please complete
legibly, preferably
in black type,or
bold block lettering**

* insert full name
of company

Note
Please read the notes
on page 2 before
completing this form.

ø insert name(s) and
address(es) of all
the directors

To the Registrar of Companies

For official use

Company number

Name of company

*

I/We ø _____

_____

_____

_____

_____

_____

_____

_____

† delete as
appropriate

[the sole director][all the directors]† of the above company do solemnly and sincerely declare that:

The business of the company is:

§ delete whichever
is inappropriate

(a) that of a [recognised bank][licensed institution]† within the meaning of the Banking Act 1979§

(b) that of a person authorised under section 3 or 4 of the Insurance Companies Act 1982 to carry on insurance business in the United Kingdom§

(c) that of something other than the above§

The company is proposing to make a payment out of capital for the redemption or purchase of its own shares

The amount of the permissible capital payment for the shares in question is £_____
(note 1)

Continued overleaf

Presentor's name address and
reference (if any):

For official Use

General Section

Post room

JORDANS

Supplied by Jordans Limited   Tel. 0117 923 0600

120

I/We have made full enquiry into the affairs and prospects of the company, and I/we have formed the opinion:

(a) as regards its initial situation immediately following the date on which the payment out of capital is proposed to be made, that there will be no grounds on which the company could then be found unable to pay its debts (note 2), and

(b) as regards its prospects for the year immediately following that date, that, having regard to my/our intentions with respect to the management of the company's business during that year and to the amount and character of the financial resources which will in my/our view be available during that year, the company will be able to continue to carry on business as a going concern (and will accordingly be able to pay its debts as they fall due) throughout that year.(note 2)

And I/we make this solemn declaration conscientiously believing the same to be true and by virtue of the provisions of the Statutory Declarations Act 1835.

Declared at _____   Declarant(s) to sign below

_____

_____

the _____ day of _____

one thousand nine hundred and _____

_____

before me _____

A Commissioner for Oaths, or Notary Public, or Justice of the Peace, or Solicitor having the powers conferred on a Commissioner for Oaths.

Notes

1 'Permissible capital payment' means an amount which, taken together with
   (i) any available profits of the company; and
   (ii) the proceeds of any fresh issue of shares made for the purposes of the redemption or purchase;
   is equal to the price of redemption or purchase.
   'Available profits' means the company's profits which are available for distribution (within the meaning of section 172 and 263 of the Companies Act 1985).
   The question whether the company has any profits so available and the amount of any such profits is to be determined in accordance with section 172 of the Companies Act 1985.

2 Contingent and prospective liabilities of the company must be taken into account, see sections 173(4) & 517 of the Companies Act 1985.

3 A copy of this declaration together with a copy of the auditors report required by section 173 of the Companies Act 1985, must be delivered to the Registrar of Companies not later than the day on which the company publishes the notice required by section 175(1) of the Companies Act 1985, or first publishes or gives the notice required by section 175(2), whichever is the earlier.

G

COMPANIES FORM No. 176

Notice of application to the Court for the cancellation of a resolution for the redemption or purchase of shares out of capital

Pursuant to section 176 of the Companies Act 1985

Please do not
write in
this margin

**Please complete
legibly, preferably
in black type, or
bold block lettering**

* insert full name
of company

To the Registrar of Companies

For official use

Company number

Name of company

*

gives notice that an application has been made to the Court for the cancellation of the special resolution

dated _____ approving payment out of capital for

the redemption or purchase of some of the company's shares.

‡ Insert
Director,
Secretary,
Administrator,
Administrative
Receiver or
Receiver
(Scotland) as
appropriate

Signed   Designation‡   Date

Presentor's name address and
reference (if any):

For official Use

General Section   Post room

JORDANS

190

Printed and supplied by

JORDANS
21 St Thomas Street Bristol BS1 6JS
Telephone: 0117 923 0600   Fax: 0117 923 0063

Please complete in typescript,
or in bold black capitals.

Location of register of debenture holders

Company Number

Company Name in full

gives notice that †[a register][registers]†[in duplicate form] of holders of
debentures of the company of the classes mentioned below †[is][are]kept at:

NOTE:
This notice is not
required where the
register is, and has
always been, kept at
the Registered Office

Address

Post town

County / region

Postcode

Brief description of class of debentures

Signed

Date

† Please delete as appropriate.

† a director / secretary

Please give the name, address,
telephone number and, if available,
a DX number and Exchange of
the person Companies House should
contact if there is any query.

Tel

DX number   DX exchange

When you have completed and signed the form please send it to the
Registrar of Companies at:
Companies House, Crown Way, Cardiff, CF4 3UZ   DX 33050 Cardiff
for companies registered in England and Wales
or
Companies House, 37 Castle Terrace, Edinburgh, EH1 2EB
for companies registered in Scotland   **DX 235 Edinburgh**

225

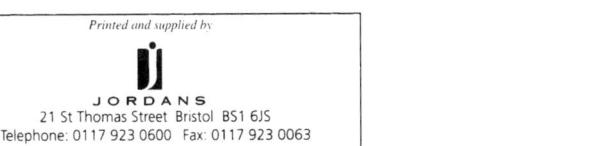

Printed and supplied by

JORDANS
21 St Thomas Street Bristol BS1 6JS
Telephone: 0117 923 0600 Fax: 0117 923 0063

Please complete in typescript,
or in bold black capitals

Change of accounting reference date

Company Number

Company Name In Full

	Day	Month	Year
The accounting reference period ending			

NOTES

You may use this form to change the accounting date relating to either the current or the immediately previous accounting period.

	Day	Month	Year
is shortened/extended† so as to end on			

a. You **may not** change a period for which the accounts are already overdue.

b. You **may not** extend a period beyond 18 months unless the company is subject to an administration order.

Subsequent periods will end on the same day and month in future years.

c. You **may not** extend periods more than once in five years unless:

If extending more than once in five years, please indicate in the box the number of the provision listed in note c. on which you are relying.

1. the company is subject to an administration order, or

2. you have the specific approval of the Secretary of State, (please enclose a copy), or

3. you are extending the company's accounting reference period to align with that of a parent or subsidiary undertaking established in the European Economic Area.

4. the form is being submitted by an oversea company.

Signed   **Date**

† Please delete as appropriate

† a director / secretary / administrator / administrative receiver / receiver and manager / receiver(Scotland) / person authorised on behalf of an oversea company

Please give the name, address, telephone number, and if available, a DX number and Exchange, for the person Companies House should contact if there is any query

Tel
DX number   DX exchange

When you have completed and signed the form please send it to the Registrar of Companies at:

Companies House, Crown Way, Cardiff, CF4 3UZ   DX 33050 Cardiff
for companies registered in England and Wales
or
Companies House, 37 Castle Terrace, Edinburgh, EH1 2EB
for companies registered in Scotland   **DX 235 Edinburgh**

Form revised 6 February 1996

COMPANIES FORM No. 244

Notice of claim to extension of period allowed for laying and delivering accounts - oversea business or interests

Please do not
write in
this margin

Pursuant to section 244 of the Companies Act 1985
as inserted by section 11 of the Companies Act 1989

**Please complete
legibly, preferably
in black type, or
bold block lettering**

To the Registrar of Companies
(**Address overleaf**)

Company number

Name of company

* insert full name
of company

*

The directors of this company give notice that the company is carrying on business, or has interests, outside the United Kingdom, the Channel Islands and the Isle of Man and claim an extension of three months to the period allowed under this section for laying and delivering accounts in relation to the financial year of the company [ending][which ended on]†

† delete as
appropriate

Day	Month	Year
		1 9

‡ Insert
Director,
Secretary,
Admininstrator,
Administrative
Receiver or
Receiver
(Scotland) as
appropriate

Signed   Designation‡   Date

Notes

1. A company which carries on business or has interests outside the United Kingdom, the Channel Islands and the Isle of Man may, by giving notice in the prescribed form to the Registrar of Companies under section 244(3) of the Act, claim an extension of three months to the period which otherwise would be allowed for the laying and delivery of accounts under section 244(1).

2. Notice must be given before the expiry of the period which would otherwise be allowed under section 244(1).

3. A separate notice will be required for each period for which the claim is made.

4. The date in the box on the form should be completed in the manner illustrated below.

0	5	0	4	1	9	8	5

Presentor's name address
telephone number and reference (if any):

For official use
D.E.B.

Post room

JORDANS

Supplied by Jordans Limited   Tel. 0117 923 0600

Notes

The address for companies registered in England and Wales or Wales is:

The Registrar of Companies
Companies House
Crown Way
Cardiff
CF4 3UZ

or, for companies registered in Scotland:

The Registrar of Companies
Companies House
100-102 George Street
Edinburgh
EH2 3DJ

Printed and supplied by

JORDANS
21 St Thomas Street Bristol BS1 6JS
Telephone: 0117 923 0600   Fax: 0117 923 0063

Please complete in typescript,
or in bold black capitals.

287

Change in situation or address of Registered Office

Company Number

Company Name in full

New situation of registered office

NOTE:

The change in the situation of the registered office does not take effect until the Registrar has registered this notice.

For 14 days beginning with the date that a change of registered office is registered, a person may validly serve any document on the company at its previous registered office.

PO Box numbers only are not acceptable.

Address

Post town

County / Region   Postcode

Signed   **Date**

† Please delete as appropriate.

† a director / secretary / administrator / administrative receiver / liquidator / receiver manager / receiver

Please give the name, address, telephone number and, if available, a DX number and Exchange of the person Companies House should contact if there is any query.

Tel

DX number   DX exchange

When you have completed and signed the form please send it to the Registrar of Companies at:
Companies House, Crown Way, Cardiff, CF4 3UZ   DX 33050 Cardiff
for companies registered in England and Wales
or
Companies House, 37 Castle Terrace, Edinburgh, EH1 2EB
for companies registered in Scotland   **DX 235 Edinburgh**

Printed and supplied by

JORDANS
21 St Thomas Street Bristol BS1 6JS
Telephone: 0117 923 0600 Fax: 0117 923 0063

288a

Please complete in typescript, or in bold black capitals.

Appointment of director or secretary

Company Number	
Company Name in full	

	Day	Month	Year		Day	Month	Year
Date of appointment				†Date of Birth			

Appointment form

Appointment as director ☐ as secretary ☐

Please mark the appropriate box. If appointment is as a director and secretary mark both boxes.

Notes on completion appear on reverse.

NAME

*Style / Title		*Honours etc	
Forename(s)			
Surname			
Previous Forename(s)		Previous Surname(s)	
Usual residential address			
Post town		Postcode	
County / Region		Country	
†Nationality		†Business occupation	
†Other directorships (additional space overleaf)			

I consent to act as ** director / secretary of the above named company

Consent signature		**Date**	

* Voluntary details.
† Directors only.

A director, secretary etc must sign the form below.

Signed		**Date**	

** Please delete as appropriate

(**a director / secretary / administrator / administrative receiver / receiver manager / receiver)

Please give the name, address, telephone number and, if available, a DX number and Exchange of the person Companies House should contact if there is any query.

	Tel
DX number	DX exchange

When you have completed and signed the form please send it to the Registrar of Companies at:

Companies House, Crown Way, Cardiff, CF4 3UZ   **DX 33050 Cardiff**
for companies registered in England and Wales   **or**
Companies House, 37 Castle Terrace, Edinburgh, EH1 2EB
for companies registered in Scotland   **DX 235 Edinburgh**

132

Company Number

† Directors only.

†Other directorships

NOTES

Show the full forenames, NOT INITIALS. If the director or secretary is a corporation or Scottish firm, show the name on surname line and registered or principal office on the usual residential line.

Give previous forenames or surname(s) except:
- for a married woman, the name by which she was known before marriage need not be given.
- for names not used since the age of 18 or for at least 20 years

A peer or individual known by a title may state the title instead of or in addition to the forenames and surname and need not give the name by which that person was known before he or she adopted the title or preceded to it.

Other directorships.

Give the name of every company incorporated in Great Britain of which the person concerned is a director or has been a director at any time in the past five years.

You may exclude a company which either is, or at all times during the past five years when the person concerned was a director, was
- dormant
- a parent company which wholly owned the company making the return, or
- another wholly owned subsidiary of the same parent company.

Printed and supplied by

JORDANS
21 St Thomas Street Bristol BS1 6JS
Telephone: 0117 923 0600 Fax: 0117 923 0063

288b

Resignation of director or secretary

Please complete in typescript,
or in bold black capitals.

Company Number

Company Name in full

Resignation form

Date of resignation

Day	Month	Year

Resignation as director ☐   as secretary ☐   *Please mark the appropriate box. If resignation is as a director and secretary mark both boxes.*

NAME   *Style / Title   *Honours etc

Please insert
details as
previously
notified to
Companies House.

Forename(s)

Surname

Day	Month	Year

†Date of Birth

If cessation is other than
resignation, please state reason

A serving director, secretary etc must sign the form below.

Signed   **Date**

* Voluntary details.
† Directors only.

(by a serving director / secretary / administrator / administrative receiver / receiver manager / receiver

Please give the name, address,
telephone number and, if available,
a DX number and Exchange of
the person Companies House should
contact if there is any query.

Tel

DX number   DX exchange

When you have completed and signed the form please send it to the
Registrar of Companies at:
Companies House, Crown Way, Cardiff, CF4 3UZ   DX 33050 Cardiff
for companies registered in England and Wales   **or**
Companies House, 37 Castle Terrace, Edinburgh, EH1 2EB
for companies registered in Scotland   **DX 235 Edinburgh**

Printed and supplied by

JORDANS
21 St Thomas Street Bristol BS1 6JS
Telephone: 0117 923 0600   Fax: 0117 923 0063

Please complete in typescript,
or in bold black capitals.

288c

Change of particulars for director or secretary

Company Number

Company Name in full

Changes of particulars form

Complete in all cases

Date of change of particulars

Day	Month	Year

Name

*Style / Title

*Honours etc

Forename(s)

Surname

† Date of Birth

Day	Month	Year

Change of name *(enter new name)* Forename(s)

Surname

Change of usual residential address
(enter new address)

Post town

County / Region   Postcode

Country

Other change   *(please specify)*

A serving director, secretary etc must sign the form below.

Signed   **Date**

* Voluntary details.
† Directors only.

(by a serving director / secretary / administrator / administrative receiver / receiver manager / receiver

Please give the name, address, telephone number and, if available, a DX number and Exchange of the person Companies House should contact if there is any query.

Tel

DX number   DX exchange

When you have completed and signed the form please send it to the Registrar of Companies at:
Companies House, Crown Way, Cardiff, CF4 3UZ   DX 33050 Cardiff
for companies registered in England and Wales   **or**
Companies House, 37 Castle Terrace, Edinburgh, EH1 2EB
for companies registered in Scotland   **DX 235 Edinburgh**

Printed and supplied by

JORDANS
21 St Thomas Street Bristol BS1 6JS
Telephone: 0117 923 0600   Fax: 0117 923 0063

*Please complete in typescript,
or in bold black capitals.*

318

Location of directors' service contracts

Company Number

Company Name in full

Address where directors' service contracts
or memoranda are available for inspection
by members.

NOTE:
Directors' service
contracts **MUST** be kept
at an address in the
country of incorporation.

This notice is not
required where the
relevant documents are
and have always been
kept at the Registered
Office.

Address

Post town

County / Region

Postcode

Signed

Date

† Please delete as appropriate.

† a director / secretary / administrator / administrative receiver / receiver manager / receiver

Please give the name, address,
telephone number and, if available,
a DX number and Exchange of
the person Companies House should
contact if there is any query.

Tel

DX number   DX exchange

When you have completed and signed the form please send it to the
Registrar of Companies at:
Companies House, Crown Way, Cardiff, CF4 3UZ   DX 33050 Cardiff
for companies registered in England and Wales
or
Companies House, 37 Castle Terrace, Edinburgh, EH1 2EB
for companies registered in Scotland   **DX 235 Edinburgh**

139

325

Please complete in typescript,
or in bold black capitals.

Location of register of directors' interests in shares etc.

Company Number

Company Name in full

The register of directors' interests in shares and/or debentures is kept at:

NOTE:
The register **MUST** be kept at an address in the country of incorporation.

This notice is not required where the register is and has always been kept at the Registered Office.

Address

Post town

County / Region

Postcode

Signed   **Date**

† Please delete as appropriate.

Please give the name, address, telephone number and, if available, a DX number and Exchange of the person Companies House should contact if there is any query.

† a director / secretary / administrator / administrative receiver / receiver manager / receiver

Tel

DX number   DX exchange

When you have completed and signed the form please send it to the Registrar of Companies at:
Companies House, Crown Way, Cardiff, CF4 3UZ   DX 33050 Cardiff
for companies registered in England and Wales
or
Companies House, 37 Castle Terrace, Edinburgh, EH1 2EB
for companies registered in Scotland   **DX 235 Edinburgh**

Printed and supplied by

JORDANS
21 St Thomas Street Bristol BS1 6JS
Telephone: 0117 923 0600   Fax: 0117 923 0063

353

*Please complete in typescript,
or in bold black capitals.*

Register of members

Company Number

Company Name in full

The register of members is kept at:

NOTE:
The register **MUST** be kept at an address in the country of incorporation.

This notice is not required where the register has, at all times since it came into existence (or in the case of a register in existence on 1 July 1948 at all times since then) been kept at the registered office.

Address

Post town

County / Region

Postcode

Signed

Date

† Please delete as appropriate.

Please give the name, address, telephone number and, if available, a DX number and Exchange of the person Companies House should contact if there is any query.

† a director / secretary / administrator / administrative receiver / receiver manager / receiver

Tel

DX number   DX exchange

When you have completed and signed the form please send it to the Registrar of Companies at:
Companies House, Crown Way, Cardiff, CF4 3UZ   DX 33050 Cardiff
for companies registered in England and Wales
or
Companies House, 37 Castle Terrace, Edinburgh, EH1 2EB
for companies registered in Scotland   **DX 235 Edinburgh**

143

*Please complete in typescript,
or in bold black capitals.*

363a

Annual Return

Company Number [   ]

Company Name in full [   ]

Date of this return *(See note 1)*
The information in this return is made up to

Day	Month	Year

Date of next return *(See note 2)*
If you wish to make your next return
to a date earlier than the anniversary
of this return please show the date here.
Companies House will then send a form
at the appropriate time.

Day	Month	Year

Registered Office *(See note 3)*
Show here the address **at the date of
this return.**

*Any change of
registered office
must be notified
on form 287.*

Post town

County / Region

Postcode

Principal business activities
(See note 4)
Show trade classification code number(s)
for the principal activity or activities.

If the code number cannot be determined,
give a brief description of principal activity.

When you have completed and signed the form please send it to the
Registrar of Companies at:
Companies House, Crown Way, Cardiff, CF4 3UZ   DX 33050 Cardiff
for companies registered in England and Wales
or
Companies House, 37 Castle Terrace, Edinburgh, EH1 2EB
for companies registered in Scotland   **DX 235 Edinburgh**

Page 1

144

Register of members (See note 5)

If the register of members is not kept at the registered office, state here where it is kept.

Post town

County / Region   Postcode

Register of Debenture holders

(See note 6)

If there is a register of debenture holders and it is not kept at the registered office, state here where it is kept.

Post town

County / Region   Postcode

Company type (See note 7)

Public limited company

Private company limited by shares

Private company limited by guarantee without share capital

Private company limited by shares exempt under section 30

Private company limited by guarantee exempt under section 30

Private unlimited company with share capital

Private unlimited company without share capital

Please mark the appropriate box

Company Secretary (see notes 8)

Details of a new company secretary must be notified on form 288a.

(Please photocopy this area to provide details of joint secretaries).

Name   * Style / Title   *Honours etc

Forename(s)

Surname

* Voluntary details.

Previous forename(s)

Previous surname(s)

Address

Usual residential address must be given. In the case of a corporation, give the registered or principal office address.

Post town

County / Region   Postcode

Country

Directors (see notes 8)

Please list directors in alphabetical order.

Details of new directors must be notified on form 288a

Name	* Style / Title	

Day Month Year

* Honours etc		Date of birth	

Forename(s)	

Surname	

Previous forename(s)	

Previous surname(s)	

Address	

Usual residential address must be given. In the case of a corporation, give the registered or principal office address.

Post town	

County / Region		Postcode	

Country		**Nationality**	

Business occupation	

Other directorships	

* Voluntary details.

Name	* Style / Title	

Day Month Year

* Honours etc		Date of birth	

Forename(s)	

Surname	

Previous forename(s)	

Previous surname(s)	

Address	

Usual residential address must be given. In the case of a corporation, give the registered or principal office address.

Post town	

County / Region		Postcode	

Country		**Nationality**	

Business occupation	

Other directorships	

146

Issued share capital *(see note 9)*
Enter details of all the shares in issue at the date of this return.

Class *(e.g. Ordinary/Preference)*	Number of shares issued	Aggregate Nominal Value *(i.e Number of shares issued multiplied by nominal value per share)*
Totals		

List of past and present members
(Use attached schedule where appropriate)
A full list is required if one was not included with either of the last two returns.
(see note 10)

There were no changes in the period ☐

	on paper	in another format
A list of changes is enclosed	☐	☐
A full list of members is enclosed	☐	☐

Elective resolutions
(Private companies only)
(See note 11)

If at the date of this return an election is in force to dispense with annual general meetings, *mark this box* ☐

If at the date of this return an election is in force to dispense with laying accounts in general meetings, *mark this box* ☐

Certificate

I certify that the information given in this return is true to the best of my knowledge and belief.

Signed [   ] **Date** [   ]

† Please delete as appropriate.

† a director /secretary

When you have signed the return send it with the fee to the Registrar of Companies. Cheques should be made payable to **Companies House.**

This return includes [   ] continuation sheets.
(enter number)

Please give the name, address, telephone number, and if available, a DX number and Exchange, for the person Companies House should contact if there is any query.

Tel
DX number   DX exchange

Details of new directors must be notified on form 288a

Directors (continued)

				Day	Month	Year
Name	* Style / Title					
	* Honours etc		Date of birth			

Forename(s)

Surname

Previous forename(s)

Previous surname(s)

Address

Usual residential address must be given. In the case of a corporation, give the registered or principal office address.

Post town

County / Region — Postcode

Country — **Nationality**

Business occupation

Other directorships

* Voluntary details

				Day	Month	Year
Name	* Style / Title					
	* Honours etc		Date of birth			

Forename(s)

Surname

Previous forename(s)

Previous surname(s)

Address

Usual residential address must be given. In the case of a corporation, give the registered or principal office address.

Post town

County / Region — Postcode

Country — **Nationality**

Business occupation

Other directorships

148

Directors (continued)

Details of new directors must be notified on form 288a

Name   * Style / Title [_____]   Day   Month   Year

* Honours etc [_____]   Date of birth [___|___|___]

Forename(s) [_____]

Surname [_____]

Previous forename(s) [_____]

Previous surname(s) [_____]

Address [_____]

[_____]

Usual residential address must be given. In the case of a corporation, give the registered or principal office address.

Post town [_____]

County / Region [_____]   Postcode [_____]

Country [_____]   **Nationality** [_____]

Business occupation [_____]

Other directorships [_____]

[_____]

* Voluntary details.

Name   * Style / Title [_____]   Day   Month   Year

* Honours etc [_____]   Date of birth [___|___|___]

Forename(s) [_____]

Surname [_____]

Previous forename(s) [_____]

Previous surname(s) [_____]

Address [_____]

[_____]

Usual residential address must be given. In the case of a corporation, give the registered or principal office address.

Post town [_____]

County / Region [_____]   Postcode [_____]

Country [_____]   **Nationality** [_____]

Business occupation [_____]

Other directorships [_____]

[_____]

Printed and supplied by

JORDANS
21 St Thomas Street Bristol BS1 6JS
Telephone: 0117 923 0600   Fax: 0117 923 0063

*Please complete in typescript,
or in bold black capitals.*

List of past and present members
Schedule to form 363a, 363b

Company Number

Company Name in full

Name and address	Number of shares or amount of stock held by existing members at date of this return.	Particulars of shares or stock transferred since the date of the last return (or in the case of the first return, since the incorporation of the company) by (a) persons who are still members, and (b) persons who have ceased to be members.		
	Number or amount currently held	Number or amount Transferred	Date of registration of transfer	Remarks

List of past and present members
Schedule to form 363a, 363b

| | Number of shares or amount of stock held by existing members at date of this return. | Particulars of shares transferred since the date of the last return or stock (or in the case of the first return, since the incorporation of the company) by (a) persons who are still members, and (b) persons who have ceased to be members. | | |
Name and address	Number or amount currently held	Number or amount of transferred	Date of registration of transfer	Remarks

Form 363a/b   Continuation Sheet

Company Number [ ]

Company Name [ ]

Company Secretary (see notes 1-5)

Details of a new company secretary must be notified on form 288a.

(Please photocopy this area to provide details of joint secretaries).

Name

* Style / Title [ ]

* Honours etc [ ]

Forename(s) [ ]

* Voluntary details.

Surname [ ]

Previous forename(s) [ ]

Previous surname(s) [ ]

Address [ ]

[ ]

Usual residential address must be given. In the case of a corporation, give the registered or principal office address.

Post town [ ]

County / Region [ ]   Postcode [ ]

Country [ ]

Directors (see notes 1-5)

Please list directors in alphabetical order

Details of new directors must be notified on form 288a.

Name

* Style / Title [ ]

	Day	Month	Year

* Honours etc [ ]   Date of birth [ ][ ][ ]

Forename(s) [ ]

Surname [ ]

Previous forename(s) [ ]

Previous surname(s) [ ]

Address [ ]

[ ]

Usual residential address must be given. In the case of a corporation, give the registered or principal office address.

Post town [ ]

County / Region [ ]   Postcode [ ]

Country [ ]

Nationality [ ]

Business occupation [ ]

Other directorships [ ]

[ ]

152

Directors (see notes 1-5)
Please list directors in alphabetical order

Details of new directors must be notified on form 288a.

Name	* Style / Title	
	* Honours etc	Date of birth — Day / Month / Year
	Forename(s)	
	Surname	
	Previous forename(s)	
	Previous surname	
Address		

Usual residential address must be given. In the case of a corporation, give the registered or principal office address.

Post town	
County / Region	Postcode
Country	

Nationality

Business occupation

Other directorships

Directors (see notes 1-5)
Please list directors in alphabetical order

Details of new directors must be notified on form 288a.

Name	* Style / Title	
	* Honours etc	Date of birth — Day / Month / Year
	Forename(s)	
	Surname	
	Previous forename(s)	
	Previous surname	
Address		

Usual residential address must be given. In the case of a corporation, give the registered or principal office address.

Post town	
County / Region	Postcode
Country	

Nationality

Business occupation

Other directorships

Notes for Completion of Annual Return – for use with Form 363s

Introduction

Every company MUST make an Annual Return to the Registrar of Companies. It is the director's duty to ensure that the return accurately reflects the affairs of the company at the date of the return.

The completed form must reach Companies House within 28 days from "the date of the return". Failure to comply is an offence.

Annual Returns are no longer linked to the date of any Annual General Meeting the company may have held.

In certain circumstances this form may be used in place of forms 190, 353, 287 and 288b or c. You should check these requirements carefully before doing so. (See notes 3, 5, 6 and 7 below.)

The information printed on this form is taken from details previously supplied to Companies House. If any of the information is incorrect or has been changed please show the correct/current information on the lined space to the right of the printed details.

If you have already notified Companies House of any changes since the form was printed, please repeat this information in the space provided.

1. Date of this return

The latest date to which this return may be made up has been pre-printed by Companies House and is either:

- the anniversary of the last return filed in accordance with the Companies Act; or

- if this is the first return of the company, the anniversary of incorporation.

You may make this return to an earlier date if you so wish by completing the date box provided, but you cannot make it to a later date. If you decide to complete the return to an earlier date than the preprinted date it must still be delivered to Companies House within **28 days of this earlier date**. If it is not delivered within 28 days a second annual return will be required made up to the "return date".

2. Date of next return

You may give, as the date of your next return, a date which is less than 12 months from the date of this return by entering the new date in the box shown. Companies House will then send your next return shortly before the date you give in this box. (The return will not show the date requested, but will show the latest date to which you may make up the return. You may then insert your required date in the box provided.) If no date is entered Companies House will send you the next annual return form shortly before the anniversary of this return.

3. Registered office

The address printed is that currently registered at Companies House. If this has been incorrectly printed or you wish to change your registered office address, please insert your new address in the space provided. This notification will serve in place of form 287.

If you wish to change your registered office address after this return has been filed you should notify the Registrar on form 287, otherwise it will not change.

4. Principal business activities

The code printed on the form is based on the Standard Industrial Classification system. If you do not agree this code or your principal activity has changed, please enter a new code or give a brief description of your activities by reference to the groups shown at the end of these notes. If you wish to add an additional code please leave the existing code intact.

5. Register of members

This section need only be completed if you do not keep the register at the registered office.

If you have changed the location of the register other than by changing the registered office please insert the location where the register is now kept.

If the register is now kept at the registered office instead of at the address printed, please mark the form "At Registered Office". This notification will serve in place of form 353.

If you change the location of the register after you have filed this return you must notify the Registrar on form 353.

6. Register of debenture holders

This section need only be completed if:

- the company has a register of debentures and

- you do not keep it (or a duplicate) at the registered office.

If the location of the register has changed from that printed on the form, please show the address of the new location.

If the register is now kept at the registered office instead of at the address printed on the form please mark the form "At Registered Office". This notification will serve in place of form 190.

If your company no longer has a register of debenture holders please mark the form "No Longer Applicable".

If you change the location of the register or duplicate after you have filed this return you must notify the Registrar on form 190.

7. Directors and secretaries

The form contains printed details of the secretary and directors of the company. If there are any corrections/changes to these details please use the lined space provided on the right of the form to show these alterations. If a person has ceased to be a secretary or director please show the date of cessation in the box provided.

The form may be used in place of form 288b or c to notify that a person has ceased to be a secretary or director, or any change in the particulars, **but it may not be used to notify an appointment. Form 288a must still be used for that purpose.**

You should note that the requirement of section 288 of the 1985 Companies Act to notify the Registrar of any change within 14 days still applies.

If you have already notified Companies House of any changes of particulars since the form was printed, please repeat this information in the space provided.

If the return does not contain details of a secretary or director previously notified to Companies House please attach a copy of the form 288a showing the appointment or, if not available, show the details on the form 288a enclosed. There is no need for the form to be signed again.

If you have failed to notify Companies House of a previous appointment please complete and have the enclosed form 288a signed. Attach a copy of it to the return and send all the documents to Companies House.

Other Directorships

A list of other directorships must be submitted with each return.

Give the name of every company incorporated in Great Britain of which the person concerned is a director or has been a director in the past 5 years. You may exclude a company which either is, or at all times during the past 5 years when the person was a director was:

- dormant,

- a parent company which wholly owned the company making the return,

- a wholly owned subsidiary of the company making the return.

- another wholly owned subsidiary of the same parent company.

If there is insufficient space on the form for other directorships you may use a separate sheet of paper which should include the company name and number together with the name of the director.

The date of birth of all directors (other than corporate bodies) must be given.

8. Issued share capital

This part applies to every company with a share capital.

For each class of shares state:

- the name of the class of shares eg ordinary / preference

- the number of shares issued to shareholders at the date of this return

- the aggregate nominal value of issued shares of that class at the date of this return.

(The aggregate nominal value of the shares is the total nominal or face value of the shares excluding any premium.)

9. **List of past and present members**

This part only applies to a company with a share capital.

Give names and addresses of all persons who hold shares or stock in the company at the date of this return and of all persons who have ceased to hold shares or stock in the company since the date of the last return.

Show

- the number of shares or amount of stock held by present members together with their addresses,

- the number of shares of each class transferred since the date of the last return (or, since the incorporation of the company if this is its first return) by current members or by persons who have ceased to be members since that date. Also show the date of registration of these transfers.

If you do not show the list of members in alphabetical order please attach an index which will help to locate any member shown on the list.

IF THIS IS YOUR FIRST RETURN YOU MUST GIVE A FULL LIST OF MEMBERS.

If you have given full details on either of the last two returns you need only include details of persons who, since the date of the last return:

- have become members,

- have ceased to be members,

- are existing members whose holding of stock or shares have changed.

Please mark "there were no changes in the period" if full details have been given on either of the last two returns and there have been no changes since.

Where the company has converted any of its shares into stock give the corresponding information in relation to that stock, stating the amount of stock instead of the number and nominal value of the shares.

Where a company has converted any of its shares to bearer warrants they should be shown as such on the return.

10. **Elective resolutions**

This part does not apply to a public company.

A private company may elect (by elective resolution):

- To dispense with the holding of annual general meetings,

- Not to lay the accounts before the company in general meeting.

You must send a copy of the resolution to the Registrar of Companies within 15 days of the passing of it.

The accounts of a company have to be delivered to Companies House even if the company has resolved that they need not be laid before it in general meeting. The accounts of a private company must normally be delivered to Companies House within 10 months after the end of the period to which they relate.

Completion of form

Please ensure that the form is complete and is signed by a director or secretary. Do not forget to enclose the fee. Cheques should be made payable to — **Companies House.**

Trade Classifications for Annual Return

UK STANDARD INDUSTRIAL CLASSIFICATION

This classification is based on the UK Standard Industrial Classification (SIC 92) Codes.

Trade Code	Group A – Agriculture, Hunting and Forestry
0111	Grow cereals & other crops
0112	Grow vegetables & nursery products
0113	Grow fruit, nuts, beverage & spice crops
0121	Farming of cattle, dairy farming
0122	Farm sheep, goats, horses, etc.
0123	Farming of swine
0124	Farming of poultry
0125	Other farming of animals
0130	Crops combined with animals, mixed farms
0141	Agricultural service activities
0142	Animal husbandry services, not vets
0150	Hunting and game rearing inc. services
0201	Forestry & logging
0202	Forestry & logging related services

Trade Code	Group B – Fishing
0501	Fishing
0502	Operation of fish hatcheries & farms

Group C – Mining & Quarrying

CA Mining & Quarrying Energy Materials

Trade Code	
1010	Mining and agglomeration of hard coal
1020	Mining and agglomeration of lignite
1030	Extraction and agglomeration of peat
1110	Extraction of petroleum & natural gas
1120	Services to oil and gas extraction
1200	Mining of uranium & thorium ores

CB Mine & Quarry, Not Energy Materials

Trade Code	
1310	Mining of iron ores
1320	Mining of non-ferrous metal ores
1411	Quarrying of stone for construction

Trade Code	Group C – Mining & Quarrying (cont)
1412	Quarry of limestone, gypsum & chalk
1413	Quarrying of slate
1421	Operation of gravel and sand pits
1422	Mining of clays and kaolin
1430	Mine chemical & fertilizer minerals
1440	Production of salt
1450	Other mining and quarrying

Group D – Manufacturing

DA Manufacture of Food; Beverages & Tobacco

Trade Code	
1511	Production and preserving of meat
1512	Production & preserve poultry meat
1513	Production meat & poultry products
1520	Process & preserve fish & products
1531	Processing & preserve potatoes
1532	Manufacture of fruit & vegetable juice
1533	Process etc. fruit, vegetables
1541	Manufacture of crude oils and fats
1542	Manufacture of refined oils & fats
1543	Manufacture margarine & similar edible fats
1551	Operation dairies & cheese making
1552	Manufacture of ice cream
1561	Manufacture of grain mill products
1562	Manufacture of starches & starch products
1571	Manufacture of prepared farm animal feeds
1572	Manufacture of prepared pet foods
1581	Manufacture of bread, fresh pastry & cakes
1582	Manufacture biscuits, preserved pastry etc.
1583	Manufacture of sugar
1584	Manufacture cocoa, chocolate, confectionery

Trade Code	Group D – Manufacturing (cont)
1585	Manufacture macaroni & similar farinaceous
1586	Processing of tea and coffee
1587	Manufacture of condiments & seasonings
1588	Manufacture of homogenised & dietetic food
1589	Manufacture of other food products
1591	Manufacture distilled potable alcoholic drinks
1592	Ethyl alcohol fermented materials
1593	Manufacture of wines
1594	Manufacture of cider & other fruit wines
1595	Manufacture other non-distilled fermented drinks
1596	Manufacture of beer
1597	Manufacture of malt
1598	Produce mineral water, soft drinks
1600	Manufacture of tobacco products

DB Manufacture of Textiles & Textile Products

Trade Code	
1711	Prepare & spin cotton-type fibres
1712	Prepare & spin woollen-type fibres
1713	Prepare & spin worsted-type fibres
1714	Preparation & spin flax-type fibres
1715	Throw & prepare silk, synthetic etc.
1716	Manufacture of sewing threads
1717	Preparation & spin of other textiles
1721	Cotton-type weaving
1722	Woollen-type weaving
1723	Worsted-type weaving
1724	Silk-type weaving
1725	Other textile weaving
1730	Finishing of textiles
1740	Manufacture made-up textiles, not apparel
1751	Manufacture of carpet & rugs
1752	Manufacture cordage, rope, twine & netting
1753	Manufacture nonwovens & goods, not apparel
1754	Manufacture of other textiles
1760	Manufacture of knitted & crocheted fabrics
1771	Manufacture of knitted & crocheted hosiery
1772	Manufacture knit & crocheted pullovers, etc.
1810	Manufacture of leather clothes
1821	Manufacture of workwear

Trade Code	Group D – Manufacturing (cont)
1822	Manufacture of other outerwear
1823	Manufacture of underwear
1824	Manufacture other wearing apparel etc.
1830	Dress & dye fur; manufacture fur articles

DC Manufacture of Leather & Leather Products

Trade Code	
1910	Tanning and dressing of leather
1920	Manufacture of luggage & the like, saddlery
1930	Manufacture of footwear

DD Manufacture of Wood & Wood Products

Trade Code	
2010	Sawmill, plane, impregnation wood
2020	Manufacture of veneer sheets, plywood, etc.
2030	Manufacture builders' carpentry & joinery
2040	Manufacture of wooden containers
2051	Manufacture of other products of wood
2052	Manufacture of articles of cork, straw etc.

DE Manufacture Paper; Publishing; Printing

Trade Code	
2111	Manufacture of pulp
2112	Manufacture of paper & paperboard
2121	Manufacture corrugated paper & containers
2122	Manufacture of household & toilet goods
2123	Manufacture of paper stationery
2124	Manufacture of wallpaper
2125	Manufacture of paper & paperboard goods
2211	Publishing of books
2212	Publishing of newspapers
2213	Publish journals & periodicals
2214	Publishing of sound recordings
2215	Other publishing
2221	Printing of newspapers
2222	Printing not elsewhere classified
2223	Bookbinding and finishing
2224	Composition and plate-making
2225	Other activities to printing
2231	Reproduction of sound recording
2232	Reproduction of video recording
2233	Reproduction of computer media

Trade Code	**Group D – Manufacturing** (cont)
	DF Manufacture Coke, Petroleum Products & Nuclear
2310	Manufacture of coke oven products
2320	Manufacture of refined petroleum products
2330	Processing of nuclear fuel
	DG Manufacture Chemicals, Prods & Man-Made
2411	Manufacture of industrial gases
2412	Manufacture of dyes and pigments
2413	Manufacture other inorganic basic chemicals
2414	Manufacture other organic basic chemicals
2415	Manufacture fertilizers, nitrogen compounds
2416	Manufacture of plastics in primary forms
2417	Manufacture synthetic rubber primary forms
2420	Manufacture of pesticides & agro-chemicals
2430	Manufacture of paints, print ink & mastics etc.
2441	Manufacture of basic pharmaceutical prods
2442	Manufacture of pharmaceutical preparations
2451	Manufacture soap & detergents, polishes etc.
2452	Manufacture perfumes & toilet preparations
2461	Manufacture of explosives
2462	Manufacture of glues and gelatines
2463	Manufacture of essential oils
2464	Manufacture photograph chemical material
2465	Manufacture of prepared unrecorded media
2466	Manufacture of other chemical products
2470	Manufacture of man-made fibres
	DH Manufacture of Rubber & Plastic Products
2511	Manufacture of rubber tyres & tubes
2512	Retread & rebuild rubber tyres
2513	Manufacture of other rubber products
2521	Manufacture of plastic plates, sheets, etc.

Trade Code	**Group D – Manufacturing** (cont)
2522	Manufacture of plastic packing goods
2523	Manufacture of builders' ware of plastic
2524	Manufacture of other plastic products
	DI Manufacture Other Non-Metal Mineral Products
2611	Manufacture of flat glass
2612	Shaping & process of flat glass
2613	Manufacture of hollow glass
2614	Manufacture of glass fibres
2615	Manufacture other glass inc. technical
2621	Manufacture of ceramic household etc. goods
2622	Manufacture of ceramic sanitary fixtures
2623	Manufacture of ceramic insulators etc.
2624	Manufacture other technical ceramic goods
2625	Manufacture of other ceramic products
2626	Manufacture of refractory ceramic products
2630	Manufacture of ceramic tiles & flags
2640	Manufacture of bricks, etc. in baked clay
2651	Manufacture of cement
2652	Manufacture of lime
2653	Manufacture of plaster
2661	Manufacture concrete goods for construction
2662	Manufacture plaster goods for construction
2663	Manufacture of ready-mixed concrete
2664	Manufacture of mortars
2665	Manufacture of fibre cement
2666	Manufacture other articles of concrete, etc.
2670	Cutting, shaping & finish stone
2681	Production of abrasive products
2682	Manufacture other non-metal mineral
	DJ Basic Metals & Fabricated Products
2710	Manufacture of basic iron & steel (ecsc)
2721	Manufacture of cast iron tubes
2722	Manufacture of steel tubes
2731	Cold drawing
2732	Cold rolling of narrow strips
2733	Cold forming or folding
2734	Wire drawing

Trade Code	**Group D – Manufacturing** (cont)
2735	Other 1st process iron & steel
2741	Precious metals production
2742	Aluminium production
2743	Lead, zinc and tin production
2744	Copper production
2745	Other non-ferrous metal production
2751	Casting of iron
2752	Casting of steel
2753	Casting of light metals
2754	Casting of other non-ferrous metals

Manufacture Fabricated Metal, Not Machines

2811	Manufacture metal structures & parts
2812	Manufacture builders' carpentry of metal
2821	Manufacture tanks, etc. & metal containers
2822	Manufacture central heating rads & boilers
2830	Manufacture steam generators, not boilers
2840	Forge press stamp & roll form metal
2851	Treatment and coat metals
2852	General mechanical engineering
2861	Manufacture of cutlery
2862	Manufacture of tools
2863	Manufacture of locks and hinges
2871	Manufacture steel drums, similar containers
2872	Manufacture of light metal packaging
2873	Manufacture of wire products
2874	Manufacture fasteners, screws, chains etc.
2875	Manufacture other fabricated metal products

DK Manufacture of Machinery & Equipment

2911	Manufacture engines, not aircraft, etc.
2912	Manufacture of pumps & compressors
2913	Manufacture of taps and valves
2914	Manufacture bearings, gears, gear etc.
2921	Manufacture of furnaces & furnace burners
2922	Manufacture of lift & handling equipment
2923	Manufacture non-domestic ventilation
2924	Manufacture of other general machinery

Trade Code	**Group D – Manufacturing** (cont)
2931	Manufacture of agricultural tractors
2932	Manufacture other agric. & forestry machines
2940	Manufacture of machine tools
2951	Manufacture of machinery for metallurgy
2952	Manufacture machines for mining, quarry etc.
2953	Manufacture for food, beverage & tobacco
2954	Manufacture for textile, apparel & leather
2955	Manufacture machinery for paper & board
2956	Manufacture other special purpose machine
2960	Manufacture of weapons & ammunition
2971	Manufacture of electric domestic appliances
2972	Manufacture non-electric domestic appliances

DL Manufacture Electrical & Optical Equipment

Manufacture of Office Machinery & Computers

3001	Manufacture of office machinery
3002	Manufacture computers & process equipment

Manufacture of Electrical Machinery etc.

3110	Manufacture electric motors, generators etc.
3120	Manufacture electricity distribution etc.
3130	Manufacture of insulated wire & cable
3140	Manufacture of accumulators, batteries etc.
3150	Manufacture lighting equipment & lamps
3161	Manufacture electric equipment, engines etc.
3162	Manufacture other electrical equipment

Manufacture of Radio, TV & Equipment

3210	Manufacture of electronic components
3220	Manufacture TV transmitters, telephony etc.
3230	Manufacture TV & radio, sound or video etc.

Trade Code	Group D – Manufacturing (cont)
	Manufacture Medical & Precision Instruments
3310	Manufacture medical, orthopaedic etc. equipment
3320	Manufacture instruments for measuring etc.
3330	Manufacture indust process control equipment
3340	Manufacture optical, photographic etc. equipment
3350	Manufacture of watches and clocks
	DM Manufacture of Transport Equipment
3410	Manufacture of motor vehicles
3420	Manufacture motor vehicle bodies etc.
3430	Manufacture motor vehicle & engine parts
	Manufacture of Other Transport Equipment
3511	Building and repairing of ships
3512	Build & repair pleasure & sport boats
3520	Manufacture of railway locomotives & stock
3530	Manufacture of aircraft & spacecraft
3541	Manufacture of motorcycles
3542	Manufacture of bicycles
3543	Manufacture of invalid carriages
3550	Manufacture other transport equipment
	DN Manufacturing nec
3611	Manufacture of chairs and seats
3612	Manufacture other office & shop furniture
3613	Manufacture of other kitchen furniture
3614	Manufacture of other furniture
3615	Manufacture of mattresses
3621	Striking of coins and medals
3622	Manufacture of jewellery & related
3630	Manufacture of musical instruments
3640	Manufacture of sports goods
3650	Manufacture of games and toys
3661	Manufacture of imitation jewellery
3662	Manufacture of brooms and brushes
3663	Other manufacturing

Trade Code	Group D – Manufacturing (cont)
	Recycling
3710	Recycling of metal waste and scrap
3720	Recycling non-metal waste & scrap
	Group E – Electricity, Gas and Water Supply
4010	Production, distribution electric
4020	Manufacture of gas; mains distribution
4030	Steam and hot water supply
4100	Collection, purify etc. of water
	Group F – Construction
4511	Demolition buildings; earth moving
4512	Test drilling and boring
4521	General construction & civil engineering
4522	Erection of roof covering & frames
4523	Construction roads, airfields etc.
4524	Construction of water projects
4525	Other special trades construction
4531	Installation electrical wiring etc.
4532	Insulation work activities
4533	Plumbing
4534	Other building installation
4541	Plastering
4542	Joinery installation
4543	Floor and wall covering
4544	Painting and glazing
4545	Other building completion
4550	Rent construction equipment with operator
	Group G – Wholesale, Retail; Certain Repair
5010	Sale of motor vehicles
5020	Maintenance & repair of motors
5030	Sale of motor vehicle parts etc.
5040	Sale, repair etc. m'cycles & parts
5050	Retail sale of automotive fuel
	Wholesale, Commission, Not Motors
5111	Agents agricultural & textile raw materials
5112	Agents in sale of fuels, ores, etc.
5113	Agents in building materials
5114	Agents in industrial equipment, etc.

Trade Code	**Group G – Wholesale, Retail; Certain Repair** (cont)
5115	Agents in household goods, etc.
5116	Agents in textiles, footwear etc.
5117	Agents in food, drink & tobacco
5118	Agents in particular products
5119	Agents in sale of variety of goods
5121	Wholesale of grain, animal feeds
5122	Wholesale of flowers and plants
5123	Wholesale of live animals
5124	Wholesale hides, skins and leather
5125	Wholesale of unmanufactured tobacco
5131	Wholesale of fruit and vegetables
5132	Wholesale of meat and meat products
5133	Wholesale dairy produce, oils etc.
5134	Wholesale alcoholic & other drinks
5135	Wholesale of tobacco products
5136	Wholesale sugar, chocolate etc.
5137	Wholesale coffee, tea, cocoa etc.
5138	Wholesale other food inc fish, etc.
5139	Non-specialised wholesale food, etc.
5141	Wholesale of textiles
5142	Wholesale of clothing and footwear
5143	Wholesale electric household goods
5144	Wholesale of china, wallpaper etc.
5145	Wholesale of perfume and cosmetics
5146	Wholesale of pharmaceutical goods
5147	Wholesale of other household goods
5151	Wholesale fuels & related products
5152	Wholesale of metals and metal ores
5153	Wholesale wood, construction etc.
5154	Wholesale hardware, plumbing etc.
5155	Wholesale of chemical products
5156	Wholesale other intermediate goods
5157	Wholesale of waste and scrap
5161	Wholesale of machine tools
5162	Wholesale of construction machinery
5163	Wholesale textile industry machines
5164	Wholesale office machinery & equipment

Trade Code	**Group G – Wholesale, Retail; Certain Repair** (cont)
5165	Wholesale machines, industry, etc.
5166	Wholesale agric. machines & tractors
5170	Other wholesale

Retail Trade, Not Motors; Repairs

5211	Retail non-special stores food, etc.
5212	Other retail non-specialised stores
5221	Retail of fruit and vegetables
5222	Retail of meat and meat products
5223	Retail of fish, crustaceans etc.
5224	Retail bread, cakes, confectionery
5225	Retail alcoholic & other beverages
5226	Retail sale of tobacco products
5227	Other retail food etc. specialised
5231	Dispensing chemists
5232	Retail medical & orthopaedic goods
5233	Retail cosmetic & toilet articles
5241	Retail sale of textiles
5242	Retail sale of clothing
5243	Retail of footwear & leather goods
5244	Retail furniture household etc.
5245	Retail electric h'hold, etc. goods
5246	Retail hardware, paints & glass
5247	Retail books, newspapers etc.
5248	Other retail specialised stores
5250	Retail second-hand goods in stores
5261	Retail sale via mail order houses
5262	Retail sale via stalls and markets
5263	Other non-store retail sale
5271	Repair boots, shoes, leather goods
5272	Repair electrical household goods
5273	Repair of clocks & jewellery
5274	Repair not elsewhere classified

Group H – Hotels and Restaurants

5511	Hotels & motels, with restaurant
5512	Hotels & motels, without restaurant
5521	Youth hostels and mountain refuges
5522	Camp sites, including caravan sites
5523	Other provision of lodgings
5530	Restaurants
5540	Bars

Trade Code	Group H – Hotels & Restaurants (cont)
5551	Canteens
5552	Catering

Group I – Transport, Storage & Communication

6010	Transport via railways
6021	Other sched passenger land transport
6022	Taxi operation
6023	Other passenger land transport
6024	Freight transport by road
6030	Transport via pipelines

Water Transport

6110	Sea and coastal water transport
6120	Inland water transport

Air Transport

6210	Scheduled air transport
6220	Non-scheduled air transport
6230	Space transport

Support Transport; Travel Agencies

6311	Cargo handling
6312	Storage and warehousing
6321	Other supporting land transport
6322	Other supporting water transport
6323	Other supporting air transport
6330	Travel agencies etc; tourist
6340	Other transport agencies

Post and Telecommunications

6411	National post activities
6412	Courier other than national post
6420	Telecommunications

Group J – Financial Intermediation

6511	Central banking
6512	Other monetary intermediation
6521	Financial leasing
6522	Other credit granting
6523	Other financial intermediation

Insurance, Pension not comp soc sec

6601	Life Insurance
6602	Pension funding
6603	Non-life insurance

Activities Aux to Financial Interm

6711	Administration of financial markets
6712	Security broking & fund management
6713	Auxiliary financial intermed

Trade Code	Group J – Financial Intermediation (cont)
6720	Auxiliary insurance & pension fund

Group K – Real Estate, Renting & Business

7011	Development & sell real estate
7012	Buying & sell own real estate
7020	Letting of own property
7031	Real estate agencies
7032	Manage real estate, fee or contract

Renting Equipment Without Operator

7110	Renting of automobiles
7121	Rent other land transport equipment
7122	Rent water transport equipment
7123	Renting of air transport equipment
7131	Rent agricultural machinery & equipment
7132	Rent civil engineering machinery
7133	Rent office machinery inc. computers
7134	Rent other machinery & equipment
7140	Rent personal & household goods

Computer and Related Activities

7210	Hardware consultancy
7220	Software consultancy and supply
7230	Data processing
7240	Data base activities
7250	Maintenance office & computing machinery
7260	Other computer related activities

Research and Development

7310	R & D on nat sciences & engineering
7320	R & D on soc sciences & humanities

Other Business Activities

7411	Legal activities
7412	Accounting, auditing; tax consult
7413	Market research, opinion polling
7414	Business & management consultancy
7415	Management activities holding comps
7420	Architectural, technical consult
7430	Technical testing and analysis
7440	Advertising
7450	Labour recruitment
7460	Investigation & security

Trade Code	Group K – Real Estate, Renting & Business (cont)
7470	Industrial cleaning
7481	Photographic activities
7482	Packaging activities
7483	Secretarial & translation
7484	Other business activities
7499	Non-trading company

Group L – Public Administration & Defence

7511	General (overall) public service
7512	Regulation health, education, etc.
7513	Regulation more efficient business
7514	Support services for government
7521	Foreign affairs
7522	Defence activities
7523	Justice and judicial activities
7524	Public security, law & order
7525	Fire service activities
7530	Compulsory social security

Group M – Education

8010	Primary education
8021	General secondary education
8022	Technical & vocational secondary
8030	Higher education
8041	Driving school activities
8042	Adult and other education

Group N – Health and Social Work

8511	Hospital activities
8512	Medical practice activities
8513	Dental practice activities
8514	Other human health activities
8520	Veterinary activities
8531	Social work with accommodation
8532	Social work without accommodation

Group O – Other Social & Personal Services

9000	Refuse disposal, sanitation etc.

Membership Organisations

9111	Business & employers organisations
9112	Professional organisations
9120	Trade unions
9131	Religious organisations
9132	Political organisations
9133	Other membership organisations

Trade Code	Group O – Other Social & Personal Services (cont)

Recreational, Cultural & Sporting

9211	Motion picture and video production
9212	Motion picture & video distribution
9213	Motion picture projection
9220	Radio and television activities
9231	Artistic & literary creation
9232	Operation of arts facilities
9233	Fair and amusement park activities
9234	Other entertainment activities
9240	News agency activities
9251	Library and archives activities
9252	Museum & preservation of history
9253	Botanical, zoos & nature reserves
9261	Operate sports arenas & stadiums
9262	Other sporting activities
9271	Gambling and betting activities
9272	Other recreational activities

Other Service Activities

9301	Wash & dry clean textile & fur
9302	Hairdressing & other beauty treatment
9303	Funeral and related activities
9304	Physical well-being activities
9305	Other service activities

Group P – Private Households with Employees

9500	Private households with employees

Miscellaneous

9600	Residents Property Management

Group Q – Extra-Territorial Organisations

9900	Extra-territorial organisations

363s

Annual Return

of company number

company name

company type

This form should be completed in black.
The information printed below is taken from Companies House records as at
If this information requires amendment use the spaces opposite.

Date of this return
The information in this return should be made up to a date not later than

If you are making the return up to an earlier date, show the date here.

Day	Month	Year

Day	Month	Year

Date of next return
If you wish to make your next return to a date earlier than the anniversary of this return please show the date here. Companies House will then send a form at the appropriate time.

Day	Month	Year

Registered Office
This is the address registered by Companies House.

Principal business activities
Trade classification is

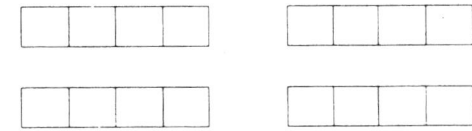

If the code number cannot be determined give a brief description of principal activity.

168

Register of members
The register is kept at

If the information shown needs amendment, give details below and, for secretary and director particulars, the date of any change.

_____
_____
_____
_____
_____

Register of debenture holders
Any register of debenture holders (or a duplicate) is kept at

_____
_____
_____
_____
_____

Company Secretary
Particulars of a new secretary **must** be notified on form 288.

Particulars

_____
_____
_____
_____
_____
_____
_____
_____
_____
_____
_____

If this person has ceased to be secretary, please state when.

Day	Month	Year

Directors
Particulars of a new director **must** be notified on form 288.

Particulars

_____
_____
_____
_____
_____
_____
_____
_____
_____
_____
_____

If this person has ceased to be a director, please state when.

Day	Month	Year

Other directorships.

_____
_____

Directors (continued)

Particulars

If the information shown needs amendment give details below and the date of any change.

If this person has ceased to be a director, please state when.

Day Month Year

Other directorships.

Particulars

If this person has ceased to be a director, please state when.

Day Month Year

Other directorships.

Particulars

If this person has ceased to be a director, please state when.

Day Month Year

Other directorships.

Issued share capital

Enter details of all shares in issue at the date of this return.

Class	Number	Aggregate nominal value
_____	_____	_____
_____	_____	_____
_____	_____	_____
_____	_____	_____
Totals		

List of past and present members

(Use attached schedule where appropriate)

A full list is required if one was not included with either of the last two returns.

Please mark the appropriate box.

There were no changes in the period ☐

	on paper	not on paper
The last full members list was at		
A list of changes is enclosed	☐	☐
A full list of members is enclosed	☐	☐

Elective resolutions

(Private companies only)

If an elective resolution is in force at the date of this return to dispense with annual general meetings, *mark this box.* ☐

If an elective resolution is in force at the date of this return to dispense with laying accounts in general meetings, *mark this box.* ☐

Certificate

I certify that the information given in this return is true to the best of my knowledge and belief.

Signed ....

Secretary/Director*
(delete as appropriate)

Date ....

This return includes .... continuation sheets.
(enter number)

To whom should Companies House direct any enquiries about the information shown in this return?

_____

_____

_____

_____ Postcode _____

Telephone _____ Ext _____

LIST OF PAST AND PRESENT MEMBERS   **SCHEDULE TO FORM 363**

Company Number:	Account of Shares		
	Number of shares or amount of stock held by existing members at date of this return.	Particulars of shares transferred since the date of the last return, or, in the case of the first return, since the incorporation of the company, by (a) persons who are still members, and (b) persons who have ceased to be members.	
Company Name:			
Name and address		Number	Date of Registration of Transfer	Remarks

Continued overleaf

172

Company Number: Company Name: Name and address	Account of Shares			
	Number of shares or amount of stock held by existing members at date of this return.	Particulars of shares transferred since the date of the last return, or, in the case of the first return, since the incorporation of the company, by (a) persons who are still members, and (b) persons who have ceased to be members.		
		Number	Date of Registration of Transfer	Remarks

Printed and supplied by

JORDANS
21 St Thomas Street Bristol BS1 6JS
Telephone: 0117 923 0600   Fax: 0117 923 0063

391

**Please complete in typescript,
or in bold black capitals.**

Notice of passing of resolution removing an auditor

Company Number

Company Name in full

Day	Month	Year

Date of resolution

Day	Month	Year

Date of removal

Details of auditor removed from office

Firm / Partnership / Individual

Address

Post town

County / Region

Postcode

Signed

Date

† Please delete as appropriate.

† a director / secretary

Please give the name, address,
telephone number and, if available,
a DX number and Exchange of
the person Companies House should
contact if there is any query.

Tel

DX number   DX exchange

When you have completed and signed the form please send it to the
Registrar of Companies at:
Companies House, Crown Way, Cardiff, CF4 3UZ   DX 33050 Cardiff
for companies registered in England and Wales
or
Companies House, 37 Castle Terrace, Edinburgh, EH1 2EB
for companies registered in Scotland   **DX 235 Edinburgh**

M

COMPANIES FORM No. 395

Particulars of a mortgage or charge

Pursuant to section 395 of the Companies Act 1985

Please do not
write in
this margin

**Please complete
legibly, preferably
in black type, or
bold block lettering**

To the Registrar of Companies

For official use

Company number

Name of company

* insert full name
of company

*

Date of creation of the charge

Description of the instrument (if any) creating or evidencing the charge (note 2)

Amount secured by the mortgage or charge

Names and addresses of the mortgagees or persons entitled to the charge

Postcode

Presentor's name address and
reference (if any):

For official Use

Mortgage Section

Post room

Time critical reference

Page 1

JORDANS

176

Short particulars of all the property mortgaged or charged

Please do not
write in
this margin

**Please complet
legibly, prefera
in black type, o
bold block lett**

Particulars as to commission allowance or discount (note 3)

Signed _____ Date _____

On behalf of [company][mortgagee/chargee]†

† delete as
appropriate

Notes

1 The original instrument (if any) creating or evidencing the charge, together with these prescribed particulars correctly completed must be delivered to the Registrar of Companies within 21 days after the date of creation of the charge (section 395). If the property is situated and the charge was created outside the United Kingdom delivery to the Registrar must be effected within 21 days after the date on which the instrument could in due course of post, and if dispatched with due diligence, have been received in the United Kingdom (section 398). A copy of the instrument creating the charge will be accepted where the property charged is situated and the charge was created outside the United Kingdom (section 398) and in such cases the copy must be verified to be a correct copy either by the company or by the person who has delivered or sent the copy to the registrar. The verification must be signed by or on behalf of the person giving the verification and where this is given by a body corporate it must be signed by an officer of that body. A verified copy will also be accepted where section 398(4) applies (property situate in Scotland or Northern Ireland) and Form No. 398 is submitted.

2 A description of the instrument, eg "Trust Deed", "Debenture", "Mortgage" or "Legal charge", etc, as the case may be, should be given.

3 In this section there should be inserted the amount or rate per cent. of the commission, allowance or discount (if any) paid or made either directly or indirectly by the company to any person in consideration of his;
    (a) subscribing or agreeing to subscribe, whether absolutely or conditionally, or
    (b) procuring or agreeing to procure subscriptions, whether absolute or conditional,
for any of the debentures included in this return. The rate of interest payable under the terms of the debentures should not be entered.

4 If any of the spaces in this form provide insufficient space the particulars must be entered on the prescribed continuation sheet.

COMPANIES FORM No. 397

Particulars for the registration of a charge to secure a series of debentures

Please do not write in this margin

Pursuant to section 397 of the Companies Act 1985

Please complete legibly, preferably in black type, or bold block lettering

To the Registrar of Companies

For official use

Company number

Name of company

*

* insert full name of company

Date of the covering deed (if any) (note 2) _____

Total amount secured by the whole series _____

_____

_____

Date of present issue _____

Amount of present issue (if any) of debentures of the series _____

Dates of resolutions authorising the issue of the series _____

Names of the trustees (if any) for the debenture holders

General description of the property charged

Continue overleaf as necessary

Presentor's name address and reference (if any):

For official Use

Mortgage Section

Post room

Time critical Reference

Page 1

JORDANS

Supplied by Jordans Limited   Tel. 0117 923 0600

178

General description of the property charged (continued)

Please do not
write in
this margin

**Please complete
legibly, preferably
in black type, or
bold block lettering**

Particulars as to commission, allowance or discount (note 3)

Signed _____ Date _____

On behalf of [company][mortgagee/chargee]†

Notes

1 Particulars should be given on this form of a series of debentures containing (or giving by reference to any other instrument) any charge to the benefit of which the debenture holders of the series are entitled pari passu. This form is to be used for registration of particulars of the entire series, and may also be used when an issue of debentures is made at the same time as the series of debentures is created. All issues of debentures made after the registration of the series with the Registrar of Companies should be notified to the Registrar on Form No. 397a.

2 The date should be given of the covering deed (if any) by which the security is created or defined

3 In this section there should be inserted the amount or rate per cent of the commission, allowance or discount (if any) paid or made either directly or indirectly by the company to any person in consideration of his
(a) subscribing or agreeing to subscribe, whether absolutely or conditionally, or
(b) procuring or agreeing to procure subscriptions, whether absolute or conditional,
for any of the debentures included in this return. The rate of interest payable under the terms of the debentures should not be entered.

4 The deed (if any) containing the charge must be delivered with these particulars correctly completed, to the Registrar within 21 days after it's execution. If there is no such deed, one of the debentures must be so delivered within 21 days after the execution of any debenture of the series.

5 If the spaces in this form are insufficient, the particulars may be continued on a separate sheet.

M COMPANIES FORM No. 397a

Particulars of an issue of secured debentures in a series

Pursuant to section 397 of the Companies Act 1985

Please do not write in this margin

Please complete legibly, preferably in black type, or bold block lettering

To the Registrar of Companies

For official use

Company number

Name of company

* insert full name of company

*

Date of present issue

Amount of present issue

Particulars as to commission, allowance or discount (note 2)

Signed _____ Date _____

† delete as appropriate

On behalf of [company][mortgagee/chargee]†

Notes

1 This form is for use when an issue is made of debentures in a series; for registration of particulars of the entire series, Form No. 397 should be used.

2 In this space there should be inserted the amount or rate percent of the commission, allowance or discount (if any) paid or made either directly or indirectly by the company to any person in consideration of his

    (a) subscribing or agreeing to subscribe, whether absolutely or conditionally, or

    (b) procuring or agreeing to procure subscriptions, whether absolute or conditional

for any of the debentures included in this return. The rate of interest payable under the terms of the debentures should not be entered.

Presentor's name address and reference (if any):

For official Use

Mortgage Section

Post room

Time Critical Reference

JORDANS

Supplied by Jordans Limited   Tel. 0117 923 0600

M

COMPANIES FORM No. 400

Particulars of a charge subject to which property has been acquired

Pursuant to section 400 of the Companies Act 1985

To the Registrar of Companies

For official use

Company number

Name of company

*

Date and description of the instrument (if any) creating or evidencing the charge (note 1)

Amount secured by the charge

Names and addresses of the persons entitled to the charge

Short particulars of the property charged

Continue overleaf as necessary

Presentor's name address and reference (if any):

For official Use

Mortgage Section

Post room

Time critical reference

JORDANS

Supplied by Jordans Limited   Tel. 0117 923 0600

182

Short particulars of the property mortgaged or charged (continued)

Date of the acquisition of the property _____

Signed _____ Designation‡ _____ Date _____

NOTES

1 A description of the instrument,
eg,"Trust Deed","Debenture", etc, as
the case may be, should be given.

2 A verified copy of the instrument
must be delivered with these
particulars correctly completed to the
Registrar of Companies within 21 days
after the date of the completion of the
acquisition of the property which is
subject to the charge. The copy must
be verified to be a correct copy either
by the company or by the person who
has delivered or sent the copy to the
registrar. The verification must be
signed by or on behalf of the person
giving the verification and where this
is given by a body corporate it must
be signed by an officer of that body. If
the property is situated and the charge
was created outside Great Britain, they
must be delivered within 21 days after
the date on which the copy of the
instrument could in due course of
post, and if despatched with due
diligence have been received in the
United Kingdom.

M

COMPANIES FORM No. 403a

Declaration of satisfaction
in full or in part
of mortgage or charge

Pursuant to section 403(1) of the Companies Act 1985

Please do not
write in
this margin

To the Registrar of Companies

For official use

Company number

Please complete
legibly, preferably
in black type or,
bold block lettering

Name of company

* insert full name
of company

*

I, _____

of _____

† delete as
appropriate

[a director][the secretary][the administrator][the administrative receiver]† of the above company, do

‡ insert a description
of the instrument(s)
creating or
evidencing the
charge, eg
'Mortgage',
'Charge',
'Debenture' etc.

solemnly and sincerely declare that the debt for which the charge described below was given has been

paid or satisfied in [**full**][**part**]†

Date and Description of charge‡ _____

Date of Registrationø _____

Name and address of [chargee][trustee for the debenture holders] _____

ø the date of
registration may be
confirmed from the
certificate

_____

Short particulars of property charged§ _____

§ insert brief
details of
property

_____

And I make this solemn declaration conscientiously believing the same to be true and by virtue of the

provisions of the Statutory Declarations Act 1835.

Declared at _____   Declarant to sign below

_____

_____

the _____ day of _____

one thousand nine hundred and _____

before me _____

A Commissioner for Oaths or Notary Public or Justice of
the Peace or Solicitor having the powers conferred on a
Commissioner for Oaths

Presentor's name address and
reference (if any):

For official Use

Mortgage Section

Post room

JORDANS

Supplied by Jordans Limited   Tel. 0117 923 0600

M

COMPANIES FORM No. 403b

Declaration that part of the property or undertaking charged (a) has been released from the charge; (b) no longer forms part of the company's property or undertaking

Pursuant to section 403(1)(b) of the Companies Act 1985

To the Registrar of Companies

For official use

Company number

Name of company

*

I, _____

of _____

[a director][the secretary][the administrator][the administrative receiver]† of the above company, do

solemnly and sincerely declare that with respect to the charge described below the part of the property

or undertaking described [has been released from the charge][has ceased to form part of the

company's property or undertaking]†

Date and description of charge ‡ _____

Date of registration ø _____

Name and address of [chargee][trustee for the debenture holders]† _____

_____

Short particulars of property or undertaking released or no longer part of the company's property or

undertaking § _____

_____

And I make this solemn declaration conscientiously believing the same to be true and by virtue of the

provisions of the Statutory Declarations Act 1835.

Declared at _____

_____

_____

the _____ day of _____

one thousand nine hundred and _____

before me _____

A Commissioner for Oaths or Notary Public or Justice of
the Peace or Solicitor having the powers conferred on a
Commissioner for Oaths

Declarant to sign below

Presentor's name address and
reference (if any):

For official Use
Mortgage Section

Post room

Printed and supplied by

JORDANS
21 St Thomas Street Bristol BS1 6JS
Telephone: 0117 923 0600 Fax: 0117 923 0063

Please complete in typescript, or in bold black capitals

652a

Application for striking off

Company Number	
Company Name In Full	

I/We as director(s) apply for this company to be struck off the register.

In the past three months the company has not:

- traded or otherwise carried on business, or changed its name;

- disposed of for value any property or rights which it would have disposed of for value in the normal course of trading or carrying on business; or

- engaged in any other activity except for the purpose of making this application, settling its affairs or meeting a statutory requirement.

This company is not the subject of, nor the proposed subject of, insolvency proceedings or a section 425 scheme.

I/We enclose the fee of £10 (made payable to Companies House).

Name	
Signed		Date	
Name	
Signed		Date	
Name	
Signed		Date	

Please give the name, address, telephone number, and if available, a DX number and Exchange of the person Companies House should contact in connection with this application

Tel	
DX number	DX exchange

When you have signed the form send it with the fee to the Registrar of Companies at:

Companies House, Crown Way, Cardiff, CF4 3UZ   **DX 33050 Cardiff**
for companies registered in England and Wales
or
Companies House, 37 Castle Terrace Edinburgh, EH1 2EB
for companies registered in Scotland   **DX 235 Edinburgh**

Form revised May 1995

188

Notes:

Guidance notes on all aspects of striking off are available from Companies House. You are advised to read them fully BEFORE completing and returning this form.

If the company ceases to be eligible for striking off at any time after the application is made, then the application must be withdrawn using form 652c. Failure to do so is an offence.

Copies of this application must be sent to all notifiable parties i.e. creditors, employees, shareholders, pension managers or trustees and other directors of the company within 7 days from the day on which the application is made. Copies must also be sent to anyone who later becomes a notifiable party within 7 days of becoming so. You should check the guidance notes which contain a full list of those who must be notified. Failure to notify interested parties is an offence. It is advisable to obtain and retain some proof of delivery or posting of copies to notifiable parties.

This form must be signed by the sole director, by both if there are two, or by the majority if there are more than two.

Printed and supplied by

JORDANS
21 St Thomas Street Bristol BS1 6JS
Telephone: 0117 923 0600   Fax: 0117 923 0063

Please complete in typescript,
or in bold black capitals

652c

Withdrawal of application for striking off

Company Number

Company Name In Full

The directors hereby withdraw the application dated

in which it was requested that this company be struck off the register.

This form can be signed by any director.

Name

Signed   Date

Please give the name, address, telephone number, and if available, a DX number and Exchange of the person Companies House should contact if there is any query.

Tel	
DX number	DX exchange

When you have signed the form send it to the Registrar of Companies at:

Companies House, Crown Way, Cardiff, CF4 3UZ   DX 33050 Cardiff
for companies registered in England and Wales
or
Companies House, 37 Castle Terrace, Edinburgh, EH1 2EB
for companies registered in Scotland   **DX 235 Edinburgh**

Form revised May 1995

THE COMPANIES ACTS 1985 TO 1989

J51

(COPY)

(1)

resolution

Company Number

of ....

.... Limited

Passed the .... day of .... 19........

At an Extraordinary General Meeting of the members of the above-named company, duly

convened and held at ....

....

on the .... day of .... 19........

the following (1)   RESOLUTION was duly passed:—

(2)

NOTES:
(1) Insert "Special" or "Extraordinary" as the case may be.
(2) This copy Resolution must be signed by the Chairman of the Meeting or a Director or the Secretary of the Company, and
    must then be filed with the Registrar of Companies within 15 days after being passed and can be sent to Jordan & Sons Ltd. for that purpose.

JORDANS

Supplied by Jordans Limited   Tel. 0117 923 0600

THE COMPANIES ACTS 1985 TO 1989

J379A

(COPY)

Company Number

Elective resolution

of ....
.... Limited

Passed the ....day of .... 19 ...

At an Extraordinary General Meeting of the members of the above-named company, duly

convened and held at ....
....

on the ....day of .... 19 ...

the following ELECTIVE RESOLUTION was passed unanimously, in person or by proxy, by all the Members entitled to attend and vote at the Meeting:-

NOTE:

This copy Resolution must be signed by the Chairman of the Meeting or a Director or the Secretary of the Company, and must then be filed with the Registrar of Companies within 15 days after being passed and can be sent to Jordan & Sons Ltd. for that purpose.

JORDANS

7.90

Supplied by Jordans Limited   Tel. 0117 923 0600

195

J324/328

THE COMPANIES ACT 1985

Notification by Director of his interests in Shares or Debentures, or any change therein pursuant to section 324 (1) and (2), and section 328 of the Act.

To _____ Limited

Date of appointment or event	Name of company (1)	Description of interest (2)	Name of registered holder	Nature of event	Price or consideration	Additional statements (3)

Dated _____ Signed _____ Name of Director _____

(1) Insert name of company whose shares or debentures are involved.
(2) Insert number or amount, and class, of shares or debentures involved.
(3) Section 325 (5) of the Act provides that the nature and extent of a director's interest must be recorded in the register if he so requires. This and other additional information should be written in this column.

SEE NOTES OVERLEAF

JORDANS

Supplied by Jordans Limited   Tel. 0117 923 0600

NOTES

These notes are offered as a guide to those completing this form but are not intended as an authoritative interpretation of the relevant provisions of the Act.

Directors and Company Secretaries are referred to the Companies Act 1985 Sections 324 to 328. Companies with a Stock Exchange listing are also referred to Sections 329 and 732 in respect of duty to notify the Stock Exchange.

1. Every person, who, or whose spouse or child under 18 years old (not being a Director), has an interest in shares or debentures in a company or its associated companies and who becomes a Director must give written notice to the Company of the subsistence of that interest within 5 "working" days (i.e. excluding Saturdays, Sundays and Bank Holidays).

2. A Director must notify the Company in writing, within 5 "working" days, of the occurrence of certain events affecting his interest in its shares or those of its associated companies, or the interest of his spouse or child under 18 years old (not being a Director). These events include:—

   (a) Events in consequence of which such an interest arises or ceases

   (b) Entering into a contract to sell any such shares or debentures

   (c) Assignment of any right to subscribe for shares or debentures of the Company

   (d) The grant of a right to subscribe for shares or debentures of an associated company, the exercise or the assignment of such right

3. See Sch 13 Part III for circumstances in which a notification obligation is not discharged. In particular notification requires:—

   (i) Where a contract to purchase or sell shares or debentures, or

   (ii) the assignment of a right to subscribe is notified the consideration must be stated, or if no consideration, that fact. Where the grant of a right to subscribe for shares or debentures in an associated company is notified, there must be stated (a) the date of grant (b) when it is exercisable (c) the consideration for the grant and (d) the subscription price. Where the exercise of such a right is notified the number of shares or debentures and the name(s) in which they are registered must be given.

4. An associated company to which these notes refer is defined as the subsidiary or holding company, or another subsidiary of the holding company of the company to which notice is to be given, but notice need not be given in respect of holdings in wholly-owned subsidiaries.

5. The relevant interests of a Director and his spouse or children are defined in Sch. 13 Part I. They include interests which subsist through the medium of certain kinds of trust or through another company controlled by the Director. They also include contracts to purchase or call for delivery of an interest, and to exercise voting rights (otherwise than as a mere proxy), and joint interests.

6. A 'Director' is defined as including a person in accordance with whose instructions the board is accustomed to act.

7. 'Child' (under 18 years old) includes step-child and adopted child.

8. In general, the period of five "working" days for fulfilment of an obligation to notify commences with the time the existence of an interest or the occurrence of an event comes to the knowledge of the Director. See Sch. 13 Part II for definition of periods, within which obligations imposed by section 324 must be fulfilled.

Statement by person ceasing to hold office as auditor

**Pursuant to section 394 of the Companies Act 1985
as inserted by section 123 of the Companies Act 1989**

Company Number

Name of Company _____

_____

Registered Office _____

_____

* delete as
appropriate

I/We* _____

of _____

_____

_____

hereby give notice in accordance with section 394 of the Companies Act 1985 that

(a) I/We confirm that in connection with my/our ceasing to hold office there are no circumstances which I/we consider should be brought to the notice of members or creditors of the company.

(b) I/We consider the following circumstances connected with my/our ceasing to hold office should be brought to the notice of the members or creditors of the company:-

Signed _____

JORDANS

Supplied by Jordans Limited   Tel. 0117 923 0600

Notes

1. Where an auditor ceases for any reason to hold office he must deposit at the Company's registered office a statement of any circumstances connected with his ceasing to hold office which he considers should be brought to the attention of the members or creditors of the company OR, if he considers that there are no such circumstances, a statement that there are none.

2. A notice of resignation is not effective unless it is accompanied by the required Statement. The Company must within 14 days of receipt of a notice of resignation send a copy of the notice to the Registrar of Companies.

3. In the case of a failure to seek re-appointment, this statement must be deposited not less than 14 days before the end of the time allowed for the next appointing auditors. In any other case (apart from resignation as to which see note 2) the statement must be deposited not later than the end of the period of 14 days beginning with the date on which he ceases to hold office.

4. If the statement is of circumstances which the auditor considers should be brought to the attention of members or creditors of the company the company must, within 14 days of deposit of the statement with it, EITHER (a) send a copy of it to every person who it is statutorily entitled to be sent copies of its accounts; OR (b) apply to the court and notify the auditor of the application.

5. Unless the auditor receives notice of such a court application before the end of a period of 21 days beginning the day on which he deposited the statement he must within a further 7 days send a copy of the statement to the Registrar of Companies.

6. If a notice of resignation is accompanied by a statement that there are circumstances which should be brought to the notice of members or creditors of the company the auditor may require the directors to convene an extraordinary general meeting of the company to consider his explanation. He may also require the company to circulate to members a written statement (of reasonable length) of the circumstances connected with his resignation and the company must state in the notice of meeting that such statement has been issued.

3. ADMINISTRATIVE RECORDS OF A PRIVATE LIMITED COMPANY

(This section is on pages 199 to 229. Contents are listed on page 5.)

(i) SHARE CERTIFICATE

General Notes

Every member of a company is entitled to a certificate specifying the shares held by him. Such certificate issued under the seal of the company is prima facie evidence of the member's title to the shares. The company must have the certificate ready for delivery to the shareholder within two months of allotment of the shares or the lodgement of properly completed transfer (sections 185 and 196).

Separate certificates should be issued for each class of shares.

If the company chooses not to have a seal or chooses not to seal share certificates, the company's Articles should be checked, to ensure that they are not thereby breached.

Procedure

Share certificates should be completed with the full name(s) of the shareholder(s) and it should be ensured that the details on a certificate correspond exactly with the entry in the register of members. If the company chooses to use its seal on share certificates, the certificate should be sealed and the sealing attested as provided by the articles of association of the company. If it chooses not to use the seal or does not have a seal, the certificate should be executed in accordance with section 36A of the Companies Act 1985, introduced by the Companies Act 1989 (for England and Wales) or in accordance with section 36B of the Companies Act 1985, as substituted by the Requirements of Writing (Scotland) Act 1995 (for Scotland). On the issue of a certificate the counterfoil should be completed and kept by the company. Appropriate cross-references should be made to the register of allotments or transfers and (if appropriate) to the register of sealings.

200

Company Number: _____ Certificate Number: _____

Shareholder: _____

Date: _____ Number of shares: _____

SHARE CERTIFICATE

Certificate Number	Number of Shares

Company Name:

Company Number:

This is to Certify that

is/are the Registered holder(s) of _____ Shares of _____ each _____ paid

in the above-named company, subject to the Memorandum and Articles of Association of the Company.

*This document is hereby executed by the Company/The Common Seal of the Company was hereto affixed in the presence of:

Director:

*Secretary/Director:

Date:

*Delete as appropriate
NO TRANSFER OF ANY OF THE ABOVE MENTIONED SHARES CAN BE REGISTERED UNTIL THIS CERTIFICATE HAS BEEN DEPOSITED AT THE REGISTERED OFFICE OF THE COMPANY

CK10.A4

(ii) REGISTER OF APPLICATIONS AND ALLOTMENTS

General Notes

A company is not required by law to maintain a register of applications and allotments, but a register has proved to be a useful link in the company's records, as it provides a continuous visual diary of the movement of the company's share capital.

The cross-referencing in the headings in this register also becomes a useful index to the several operations relating to share transactions.

Under the Companies Act 1985:–

(a) shares cannot be allotted by the directors unless so authorised by the articles of association or an ordinary resolution of the company in general meeting. A copy of such resolution must be filed with the Registrar of Companies (section 80); this authority may be extended if the company adopts the relevant elective regime under section 80A;

(b) any new issue of equity shares for cash must first be offered to existing shareholders pro-rata to their shareholdings. This requirement may be excluded by the memorandum or articles of association or by a special resolution of the company (sections 89 to 91 and 95);

(c) shares may not be allotted at a discount (section 100).

The restrictions under section 101 as to minimum payment on allotment and sections 99 and 102 to 104 as to payment of non-cash consideration apply only to a public company.

Numbering of Shares (section 182)

Provided that shares are issued fully paid up and ranking pari passu with all other shares in the same class it is unnecessary to number them. If numbered shares are issued they may subsequently be unnumbered by ordinary resolution of the company if fully paid up and ranking pari passu.

Under current practice, shares are usually allotted unnumbered.

Register of Applications and Allotments

Class of Shares _____

Entry No	Date of Application	Date of Allotment	Name of Applicant	Number of Shares		Price per Share	Amount paid	Allotted for consideration other than cash	Number of		Entered in Register of Members	Remarks
				Applied for	Allotted				Allotment Letter	Share Certificate		

CK 1

(iii) REGISTER OF TRANSFERS

General Notes

A company is not required by law to keep a register of transfers of shares, but such a register has proved to be a very useful and necessary adjunct to the records of a company, and will assist in the preparation of annual returns.

The register provides a continuous visual diary and indicator of share transfers.

The cross-referencing in the headings of the register also becomes an index to the several related operations.

It is no longer essential for a private company to restrict the free transferability of its shares, but any restriction that may be in the articles must be observed.

If the 1985 'Table A' Articles of Association apply (regulation 23) and the shares are fully paid the transfer need only be executed by the transferor(s). If not fully paid the transferee(s) must also execute the transfer.

If the company refuses to register a transfer, it must send the transferee a notice of refusal within two months of the date on which the transfer was lodged (section 183(5)).

Stamping of Transfers, etc

It is not lawful for the company to register a transfer unless a proper instrument of transfer has been delivered to it, ie the transfer deed must bear *ad valorem* duty or such amount indicated by adjudication or denoting stamp of the Inland Revenue, or be properly certified as exempt from duty.

The form of certificate and the details of exemptions from *ad valorem* duty are set out on the reverse of form J30. It will be noted that there are three classes of exemption (i) exemption certificate by completion of certificate; (ii) exemption after adjudication by the Stamp Office of the Inland Revenue; (iii) fixed duty 50p only payable (see Instructional Notes on reverse of form J30 at page 206).

Note that stamp duty is payable *ad valorem* on the purchase by a company of its own shares. See form 169 on page 117.

Register of Transfers

Transfer No.	Date of Registration	Transferee					Transferor		Balance Certificate		Sealing Register Reference
		Name	No of Shares acquired	Price or Consideration	No. of Share Certificate	Sealing Register Reference	Name	No of Shares for which certificate surrendered	No. of Shares	Certificate No.	

CK 2

STOCK TRANSFER FORM

J30

(Above this line for Registrars only)

Certificate lodged with the Registrar

Consideration Money £ . . . .

(For completion by the Registrar/Stock Exchange)

Full name of Under-taking.	
Full description of Security.	

Number or amount of Shares, Stock or other security and, in figures column only, number and denomination of units, if any.

Words

Figures

(units of   )

Name(s) of registered holder(s) should be given in full; the address should be given where there is only one holder.

If the transfer is not made by the registered holder(s) insert also the name(s) and capacity (e.g., Executor(s)) of the person(s) making the transfer.

In the name(s) of

Account Designation (if any)

I/We hereby transfer the above security out of the name(s) aforesaid to the person(s) named below *or to the several persons named in Parts 2 of Brokers Transfer Forms relating to the above security:*

Delete words in italics except for stock exchange transactions.

Signature(s) of transferor(s)

1. . . . .

2. . . . .

3. . . . .

4. . . . .

A body corporate should execute this transfer under its common seal or otherwise in accordance with applicable statutory requirements.

Stamp of Selling Broker(s) or, for transactions which are not stock exchange transactions, of Agent(s), if any, acting for the Transferor(s).

Date . . . .

PLEASE SIGN HERE

Account Designation (if any)

Full name(s) and full postal address(es) (including County or, if applicable, Postal District number) of the person(s) to whom the security is transferred.

Please state title, if any, or whether Mr., Mrs. or Miss.

Please complete in typewriting or in Block Capitals.

I/We request that such entries be made in the register as are necessary to give effect to this transfer.

Stamp of Buying Broker(s) (if any)	Stamp or name and address of person lodging this form (if other than the Buying Broker(s))

Reference to the Registrar in this form means the registrar or registration agent of the undertaking, not the Registrar of Companies at Companies House.

JORDANS

Supplied by Jordans Limited   Tel. 0117 923 0600

7.96

FORM of CERTIFICATE REQUIRED WHERE TRANSFER IS NOT LIABLE TO STAMP DUTY
Pursuant to the Stamp Duty (Exempt Instruments) Regulations 1987

(1) Delete as appropriate
(2) Insert "A", "B" or appropriate category

(1) I/We hereby certify that this instrument falls within category(2)_____ in the schedule to the Stamp Duty (Exempt Instruments) Regulations 1987, set out below.

*Signature(s)

*Description: "Transferor", "Solicitor", or state capacity of other person duly authorised to sign and giving the certificate from his known knowledge of the transaction.

_____

_____

_____

_____

_____

_____

Date _____ 19 _____

*NOTE — The above certificate should be signed by (i) the transferor(s) or (ii) a solicitor or other person (e.g. bank acting as trustee or executor) having a full knowledge of the facts. Such other person must state the capacity in which he signs, that he is authorised so to sign and gives the certificate from his own knowledge of the transaction.

SCHEDULE

A. The vesting of property subject to a trust in the trustees of the trust on the appointment of a new trustee, or in the continuing trustees on the retirement of a trustee.

B. The conveyance or transfer of property the subject of a specific devise or legacy to the beneficiary named in the will (or his nominee).

C. The conveyance or transfer of property which forms part of an intestate's estate to the person entitled on intestacy (or his nominee).

D. The appropriation of property within section 84(4) of the Finance Act 1985 (death: appropriation in satisfaction of a general legacy of money) or section 84(5) or (7) of that Act (death: appropriation in satisfaction of any interest of surviving spouse and in Scotland also of any interest of issue).

E. The conveyance or transfer of property which forms part of the residuary estate of a testator to a beneficiary (or his nominee) entitled solely by virtue of his entitlement under the will.

F. The conveyance or transfer of property out of a settlement in or towards satisfaction of a beneficiary's interest, not being an interest acquired for money or money's worth, being a conveyance or transfer constituting a distribution of property in accordance with the provisions of the settlement.

G. The conveyance or transfer of property on and in consideration only of marriage to a party to the marriage (or his nominee) or to trustees to be held on the terms of a settlement made in consideration only of the marriage.

H. The conveyance or transfer of property within section 83(1) of the Finance Act 1985 (transfers in connection with divorce etc.).

I. The conveyance or transfer by the liquidator of property which formed part of the assets of the company in liquidation to a shareholder of that company (or his nominee) in or towards satisfaction of the shareholder's rights on a winding-up.

J. The grant in fee simple of an easement in or over land for no consideration in money or money's worth.

K. The grant of a servitude for no consideration in money or money's worth.

L. The conveyance or transfer of property operating as a voluntary disposition *inter vivos* for no consideration in money or money's worth nor any consideration referred to in section 57 of the Stamp Act 1891 (conveyance in consideration of a debt etc.).

M. The conveyance or transfer of property by an instrument within section 84(1) of the Finance Act 1985 (death: varying disposition).

Instructional Notes

1. In order to obtain exemption from Stamp Duty on transactions described in the above schedule the Certificate must be completed and may then be lodged for registration or otherwise acted upon. Adjudication by the Stamp Office is not required.

2. This form does not apply to transactions falling within categories (a) and (b) in the form of certificate required where the transfer is not liable to ad valorem stamp duty set out below. In these cases the form of certificate printed below should be used. Transactions within either of those categories require submission of the form to the Stamp Office and remain liable to 50p duty.

FORM OF CERTIFICATE REQUIRED WHERE TRANSFER IS NOT LIABLE TO
AD VALOREM STAMP DUTY

Instruments of transfer are liable to a fixed duty of 50p when the transaction falls within one of the following categories:-

a   Transfer by way of security for a loan or re-transfer to the original transferor on repayment of a loan.

b   Transfer, not on sale and not arising under any contract of sale and where no beneficial interest in the property passes: (i) to a person who is a mere nominee of, and is nominated only by, the transferor; (ii) from a mere nominee who has at all times, held the property on behalf of the transferee; (iii) from one nominee to another nominee of the same beneficial owner where the first nominee has at all times held the property on behalf of that beneficial owner. (NOTE -- This category does not include a transfer made in any of the following circumstances: (i) by a holder of stock, etc., following the grant of an option to purchase the stock, to the person entitled to the option or his nominee; (ii) to a nominee in contemplation of a contract for the sale of the stock, etc., then about to be entered into; (iii) from the nominee of a vendor, who has instructed the nominee orally or by some unstamped writing to hold stock, etc., in trust for a purchaser, to such a purchaser.)

(1)   _____ hereby certify that the transaction in respect of which this transfer is made is one which falls within the category (2)   _____ above.

(1) "I" or "We".
(2) Insert "(a)" or "(b)"
(3) Here set out concisely the facts explaining the transaction. Adjudication may be required.

(3) _____

_____

_____

_____

*Signature(s)   *Description ("Transferor", "Solicitor", etc.)

_____   _____

_____   _____

_____   _____

_____   _____

Date _____ 19 _____

*NOTE — The above certificate should be signed by (1) the transferor(s) or (2) a member of a stock exchange or a solicitor or an accredited representative of a bank acting for the transferor(s); in cases falling within (a) where the bank or its official nominee is a party to the transfer, a certificate, instead of setting out the facts, may be to the effect that "the transfer is excepted from Section 74 of the Finance (1909-10) Act 1910". A certificate in other cases should be signed by a solicitor or other person (e.g. a bank acting as trustee or executor) having a full knowledge of the facts.

(iv) REGISTER OF MEMBERS

Content (section 352)

The information to be entered in the register is prescribed in section 352. The register may also record non-statutory information if so desired, eg dividend instructions.

Where Kept (section 353)

If the register is kept at a place other than the registered office of the company the Registrar of Companies MUST BE NOTIFIED within 14 days of the place, or any change in the place, where the register is kept. Form 353 is used for this purpose.

Commencement and Cessation of Membership

Except for the subscribers to the memorandum of association, a person does not become a member (shareholder) in a company until he has agreed to become a member and his name has been entered in the register of members, or cease to be a member until a like entry has been made transferring out his shares. The secretary must, therefore, ensure that all duly authorised changes in membership are recorded promptly in the appropriate registers, subject to the prior stamping of the relevant instrument, or an appropriate certification.

Single Member Company (section 352A)

If the number of members of a private company falls to one, the name and address of the sole member must be entered in the register, with a statement that the company has only one member and the date on which that occurred. If in such a case there is subsequently an increase to two or more members, a statement that the company has ceased to have only one member and the date of that happening must be entered on the register, with the name and address of the person who was formerly the sole member.

Inspection (section 356)

The register must be open to the inspection of any member of the company, without charge, AND likewise to any other person on payment of the prescribed fee.

Copies of the Register (section 356)

A copy of the register, or any part of it, must be furnished within 10 days of a request by a member, or any other person, on payment of the prescribed fee.

Index (section 354)

Unless the sheets in the register are arranged alphabetically so as to constitute in itself an index, every company having in excess of 50 members must also maintain with the register an index of members.

Register of Members

Name
Address

Dividends to

Class of share
Denomination
Date of entry as member
Date of cessation of membership

Date of entry of Issue or Transfer	References in Register		No of Share Certificate	Amount paid or agreed to be considered as paid	Acquisitions	Disposals	Balance	Remarks
	Allotments	Transfers						

(v) REGISTER OF DIRECTORS

Content (section 288)

The information to be entered in this register is prescribed in section 288 and particularised in section 289, as amended and now includes, in all circumstances, date of birth. This must also be shown on form 288a on the director's appointment and in the Annual Return.

Where Kept (section 288(1))

The Register MUST be kept at the registered office of the company.

Inspection (section 288(3))

The register must be open to the inspection of any member of the company without charge AND likewise to any other person on payment of the prescribed fee.

Definition of Director (section 741)

'Director' includes any person occupying the position of director by whatever name called. 'Shadow Director' means any person in accordance with whose directions or instructions the directors of the company are accustomed to act and such person shall be deemed to be a director and officer of the company. A company can be a director of another company.

An alternate director is deemed for all purposes to be a director of the company and, unless already a director, particulars should be entered in the register of directors, but endorsed 'Alternate Director'.

Particulars of 'Other Directorships' (section 289 *et seq*)

Here must be recorded other directorships at present held or which have been held by the director during the preceding five years. It is NOT necessary (section 289(3)) to record directorships in:

(a) a company of which this company is the wholly owned subsidiary;

(b) companies which are the wholly owned subsidiaries either of this company OR of another company of which this company is the wholly owned subsidiary;

(c) companies which are dormant (defined in section 250(3));

(d) oversea companies.

The expression 'company' for these purposes includes any body corporate incorporated in Great Britain AND a body corporate shall be deemed to be the wholly owned subsidiary of another if it has no members except that other AND that other's wholly owned subsidiaries and its or their nominees.

Sole Director (section 283(2))

A sole director cannot also be secretary of the company.

Changes of Directors and Particulars (section 288(2))

Any changes of directors, including alternate directors, or in the particulars in this register must be notified to the Companies Registry in the prescribed form (form 288a for appointment, form 288b for resignation etc or form 288c for change of particulars) within 14 days of the occurrence.

Form 288a, and also forms 363a and 363s (Annual Return) must carry details of directorships held within the preceding five years.

Register of Directors

Other Directorships		Date of resignation

Surname _____
(or Corporate Name if appropriate)

Forename(s) _____

Any former Forenames or Surnames _____

Residential Address _____
(or Registered or Principal Office if appropriate)

_____

_____

Nationality _____

Date of Birth _____

Business Occupation _____

DATES OF:

Appointment _____ Resignation or Cessation _____

Minute _____ Minute _____

Filing Particulars _____ Filing Particulars _____

GK1 A4

(vi) REGISTER OF SECRETARIES

Content (section 288)

The information to be entered in this register is prescribed by section 288 and particularised in section 290, as amended.

Where Kept (section 288(1))

The register MUST be kept at the registered office of the company.

Inspection (section 288(3))

The register must be open to the inspection of any member of the company without charge AND likewise to any other person on payment of the prescribed fee.

Generally

A director may be secretary of the company but a sole director cannot also be secretary (section 283(2)).

Where all the partners in a firm are joint secretaries, the name and principal office of the firm may be stated in the register instead of the detailed particulars of the names, etc, of those partners (section 290(2)). A company can be the secretary.

Anything required or authorised to be done by or to the secretary may, if the office is vacant, OR for any other reason there is no secretary capable of acting, be done by or to any assistant or deputy secretary, OR if there is no assistant or deputy secretary capable of acting, by or to any officer of the company authorised generally or specially in that behalf by the directors (section 283(3)).

The secretary of a private company is not subject to the qualification provisions of section 286.

Changes of Secretary and of Particulars (section 288(2))

Any changes of secretary or joint secretaries or in the particulars in this register must be notified to the Companies Registry in the prescribed form (form 288a for appointment, form 288b for resignation etc or form 288c for changes of particulars) within 14 days of the occurrence.

Register of Secretaries

Surname _____
(or Corporate Name if appropriate)

Forename(s) _____

Any former Forenames or Surnames _____

Residential Address _____
(or Registered or Principal Office if appropriate)

DATES OF:

Appointment _____ Resignation or Cessation _____

Minute _____ Minute _____

Filing Particulars _____ Filing Particulars _____

Surname _____
(or Corporate Name if appropriate)

Forename(s) _____

Any former Forenames or Surnames _____

Residential Address _____
(or Registered or Principal Office if appropriate)

DATES OF:

Appointment _____ Resignation or Cessation _____

Minute _____ Minute _____

Filing Particulars _____ Filing Particulars _____

(vii) REGISTER OF DIRECTORS' INTERESTS

Content (section 325)

All information received by the company from a director pursuant to section 324 must be entered in the register (section 325(2)).

The NATURE AND EXTENT of an interest recorded in the said register of a director in any shares or debentures must, IF THAT DIRECTOR SO REQUIRES, also be recorded in the Register (Sch 13, para 23) in respect of that interest.

AT ITS OWN INITIATIVE the company is required to enter details of any grant to a director of a right to subscribe for shares or debentures of the company (section 325(3)) AND the exercise of such a right (section 325(4)).

A separate register page will be kept for each director, even if it remains blank, thus making a positive statement that no interest has been notified.

Where Kept (Sch 13, Part IV)

If the register is kept at a place other than the registered office of the company the Registrar of Companies must be notified of the place, or any change in the place, where the register is kept. Form 325 is used for this purpose.

The Directors' Obligations

Section 324 and Sch 13, Part II imposes a statutory obligation upon all directors to notify the company within five days, in writing, of any interests they have in shares or debentures of:–

the company; OR

any other company which is its holding company; OR

any other company which is its subsidiary company or a subsidiary company of its holding company unless (in both cases) the company is a wholly owned subsidiary.

See Sch 13, Part III as to effective discharge of obligations.

Interests extend to directors' spouses and their children under 18.

Notification must be made upon appointment. All changes in existing interests or any new interest must be notified subsequently within the time-limit above.

Definition of Interest

It would not serve any useful purpose to attempt a generalisation of this complex subject. Comprehensive rules of definition are laid down in sections 324 to 328 and interpreted in Sch 13, Part I.

Definition of Director (section 741)

'Director' includes any person occupying the position of director by whatever name called. 'Shadow director' means a person in accordance with whose directions or instructions the directors of a company are accustomed to act. The duty to disclose interests attaches to shadow directors as well as directors (section 324(6)).

Obligations as to Entries in Register

Entries in respect of each director must be made in date order and within three working days of receipt of the information OR the granting or exercise of a right (Sch 13, Part IV).

Inspection (section 326 and Sch 13, Part IV)

The register must be open to the inspection of any member of the company without charge AND likewise to any other person on payment of the prescribed fee.

Copies of the Register (Sch 13, Part IV)

A copy of the register, or any part of it, must be sent within 10 days of a request by a member, or any other person on payment of the prescribed fee.

Production of Register at Annual General Meeting (Sch 13, Part IV)

If the company holds an annual general meeting, the register must be produced at the commencement of the meeting and remain open and accessible during the continuance of the meeting to any person attending the meeting.

Register of Directors' Interests

Name & address of person interested						Classes of share capital or debenture (a) _____ (b) _____			

Entry		Date of		Nature of Event	No of shares involved		No of shares in which interested after event	Price or consideration	Remarks
No	Date	Event	Notification		Acquisitions	Disposals			

(viii) REGISTER OF MORTGAGES AND CHARGES

Content

This register, to be maintained by the company, must not be confused with the separate register maintained at the Companies Registry by the Registrar of Companies (sections 401 and 417 (Scotland)).

Every company MUST keep its own register of charges EVEN IF NO ENTRIES ARE REQUIRED TO BE MADE IN IT. This is because of the right of inspection given to members, creditors and other persons who are thus able to see whether or not the company has created a charge on any of its assets (sections 407 or 408).

The entries required in the company's own register are in respect of all charges specifically affecting the property of the company, AND all floating charges on the undertaking or any property of the company. These would (in England) include an equitable charge in favour of a bank with whom a company has lodged documents by way of security for a loan or overdraft (but in Scotland, lodging of title deeds creates no security and so does not require registration).

The prescribed particulars of a charge and the original instrument creating it must be filed at the Companies Registry within 21 days after the date of its creation if it comes within the categories specified in sections 396 and 410(4) (Scotland). The original will be returned. Forms M395 or M400 will be used according to circumstances. The Registrar will not accept registration of a charge unless the forms are correctly completed in all particulars.

In Scotland, Forms M410 (Scot) or M416 (Scot) are used and M466 (Scot) in respect of alterations to a floating charge.

If the charges are not so registered within 21 days they are void (sections 395 and 410 (Scotland)).

When a registered charge is cancelled in full or in part the Companies Registry shall be notified by filing a Memorandum of Satisfaction (Form M403a). If part of the property charged has been released from the charge or no longer is an asset of the company Form 403b is used. In Scotland, Form 419a (Scot) or Form 419b (Scot) is used.

Where Kept (sections 407 and 422 (Scotland))

The register MUST be kept at the registered office of the company.

England

The expression "England" is used in this context to define the jurisdiction and includes Wales. The registration of charges by companies registered in England is governed by the Companies Act 1985, sections 395 to 409.

Scotland

The registration of charges by companies registered in Scotland is governed by the Companies Act 1985, sections 410 to 424.

Instruments Creating Charges (sections 406 and 421 (Scotland)).

A copy of every instrument creating a registrable charge MUST ALSO be kept at the registered office of the company.

In the case of a series of uniform debentures, a copy of one debenture of the series only is sufficient.

Inspection of Register and Documents (sections 408 and 403 (Scotland))

The register, AND a copy of any instrument creating a registrable charge, MUST be open to the inspection of any creditor or member of the company without charge AND likewise to any other person on payment of the prescribed fee.

Companies Act 1989
The Companies Act 1989 includes detailed and substantive changes to the law governing charges. However, the relevant sections have not yet come into force and have been the subject of debate and consultation. As a result all references to the Companies Act 1985 in the above paragraphs are to that Act PRIOR to the proposed amendments in the Companies Act 1989. It now appears that the proposed amendments will not be brought into force in their current form.

Register of Mortgages and Charges

Entry No.	Particulars of Charges		Amount of Charge	Rate of interest	Description of property charged	Name and address of persons entitled to Charge	Date of discharge of Charge	Remarks and date of filing
	Date	Description of Instrument creating Charge						

(ix) REGISTER OF SEALINGS AND DOCUMENTS EXECUTED

General Notes

A company is not required by law to keep a register of sealings, but such a register has proved to be a very useful adjunct to the records of a company.

Every company may choose whether to have, or to use, a common seal. If it chooses to have a common seal the company must have its name engraved on it in legible characters (section 350(1)).

The seal should be kept in safe custody at all times and be used only with the authority of the directors.

If the company uses a common seal in respect of any document, it should be affixed only in the manner allowed by the articles of association of the company, which commonly provide that documents to which the seal is affixed shall be attested by two directors, OR by a director and the secretary. Every care should be taken to ensure that the description of the document sealed will be sufficient to identify that document beyond doubt. As an added precaution against substitution it is advisable to endorse the document with the consecutive number of the entry in the sealings register.

Time of Entry in the Register

Entries SHOULD ALWAYS be made, and authenticated, at the time of affixing the seal.

Duplicate Seal (sections 39 and 40)

When a company has power in its Memorandum to transact business abroad it may, if its articles allow and it has a common seal, have an 'official' seal for use in any place outside the United Kingdom. Such official seal must be a facsimile of its common seal, but with the addition on its face of the name of every territory, district or place where it is to be used.

A company may also have a duplicate seal for the sealing of share certificates and other securities issued by the company. It must be a facsimile of its common seal, with the addition of the word 'securities'.

Execution of Deeds Abroad (section 38)

A company may, by writing under its common seal, empower any person, either generally or otherwise, as its attorney, to execute deeds on its behalf in any place outside the United Kingdom.

Execution of Documents Without Using Seal (section 36A)

If the company does not use a common seal in respect of any document, the document must be executed in accordance with section 36A of the Companies Act 1985, inserted by section 130 of the Companies Act 1989 (for England and Wales), or in accordance with section 36B of the Companies Act 1985, as substituted by the Requirements of Writing (Scotland) Act 1995 (for Scotland).

Documents expressed to be executed by the company and signed by a director and the secretary or any two directors have the same effect as if executed under seal. If the document makes clear on its face that it is intended by those making it to be a deed, it shall be regarded as such. It is sensible practice to record such documents executed by the company in a similar manner to sealings (and if a seal is also in use, differentiate them by their references, from documents sealed).

Register of Sealings and Documents Executed

Consecutive No		Date	Description of documents sealed or executed	Date of Minute	Persons attesting sealing/execution
Sealing	Executed under S 36A or S 36B				

CKR A4

(x) MINUTES

Statutory Requirements (section 382(1))

Every company MUST keep minutes of proceedings of general meetings of the company AND of its directors.

Permanent Record

The minutes are the permanent record of business transacted at a meeting and must be absolutely impartial.

They must record the DECISIONS reached at a meeting, and be expressed in clear and unambiguous terms. Special care should be taken to record relevant dates and figures.

Minutes, when signed by the chairman of the meeting, or by the chairman of the next succeeding meeting, are prima facie evidence of the proceedings (section 382(2)).

Security

Loose-leaf minute books are permissible, but for security reasons adequate precautions MUST be taken to guard against falsification and to facilitate discovery (section 722(2)).

For added protection each page of minutes should be initialled in the box provided at the foot of the page.

Separate Records

It is preferable to keep the minutes of general meetings separated from those of directors' meetings, because members have a right to inspection of the former.

Where Kept (section 383(1)).

The minutes of proceedings of all general meetings MUST be kept at the registered office of the company.

Inspection (section 383(2))

Minutes of general meetings of the company MUST be open to the inspection of any member of the company without charge.

Copies of Minutes (section 383(3))

Copies of any minutes of a general meeting MUST be supplied within seven days after a request by a member upon payment of the prescribed fee.

Written Resolutions of the Company (section 382A)

When a written resolution is used in accordance with section 381A instead of a meeting of the company being held, the provisions of section 382A must be followed.

A record of the resolution (and of the signatures) must be entered in the minute book and if signed by a director or the company secretary is evidence of the proceedings in agreeing to the resolution.

Written Resolutions of the Directors

Written resolutions of the directors in lieu of a meeting must conform with any special provisions of the Articles of Association or regulation 93 in Table A (1985) if applicable.

Minutes

Subject Heading:

Initial

CK9 F8-88

4. DOCUMENTS TO BE FILED AT THE COMPANIES REGISTRY IN RESPECT OF A FOREIGN COMPANY WHICH ESTABLISHES A PLACE OF BUSINESS OR A BRANCH IN GREAT BRITAIN

(This section is on pages 231 to 274. Contents are listed on pages 5 and 6.)

Introduction

Part XXIII of the Companies Act 1985 (sections 690A to 705A), as amended by the Oversea Companies and Credit and Financial Institutions (Branch Disclosure) Regulations 1992 (SI 1992 No 3179), contains detailed provisions *applicable to foreign companies which establish a place of business or a branch in Great Britain*, requiring them to deliver documents and information to the appropriate companies registry.

There are two separate sets of requirements, normally referred to as the 'branch registration regime' and the 'place of business registration regime'. The rules governing whether one regime or the other (or neither) applies are extremely complex and are not detailed here. Reference should be made to the appropriate sections and guidance notes.

Place of Business Registration Regime

If registering under the place of business regime, the relevant documents to be delivered are:

   (i) form 691;
   (ii) a certified copy of the instrument which defines the company's constitution together with a certified translation of it if it is not in English;
   (iii) the registration fee.

The provisions applicable to establishing a financial year, accounting reference periods and an accounting reference date for a company incorporated under the Companies Act 1985 (sections 223 to 225) apply to an oversea company which establishes a place of business, with appropriate modifications. Form 225 (see page 125) can be used to alter the accounting reference date.

Continuing filing requirements under this regime include the filing of accounts in respect of each financial year of the company, prepared in accordance with the Oversea Companies (Accounts) (Modifications and Exemptions) Order 1990 (SI 1990 No 440). These do not need to be audited. A fee is payable on filing.

The provisions in the Companies Act 1985 relating to the registration of charges also apply to charges on property in England and Wales (or Scotland) created, and to charges on property in England and Wales (or Scotland) acquired, by a company which has established a place of business in England and Wales (or Scotland). The same forms as prescribed for English and Welsh (or Scottish) companies are used.

Changes to details registered under the place of business regime must be notified on forms 692(1)(a), 692(1)(b), 692(1)(c) and 692(2) as appropriate.

A company must notify the Companies Registry when it ceases to have any place of business. There is no prescribed form.

Branch Registration Regime

If registering under the branch regime, the relevant documents to be delivered are:

(i) form BR1;
(ii) a certified copy of the instrument which defines the company's constitution, together with a certified translation of it if it is not in English (unless previously filed at that registry in respect of another branch);
(iii) the registration fee.

Continuing filing requirements under this regime include the filing of accounts. If the law of the country in which the foreign company is incorporated requires it to disclose audited accounts, copies should be filed with the Companies Registry within three months of such disclosure. If the law of the country in which the foreign company is incorporated has no such requirement, the provisions applicable to oversea companies registered under the place of business regime will apply. A fee is payable on filing.

The provisions regarding registration of certain charges, etc, applicable under the place of business regime also apply to a foreign company which registers a branch.

Changes to details registered under the branch regime must be notified on forms BR2, BR3, BR4, BR5 or BR6, as appropriate. If the company wishes to change the branch at which the constitutional documents have been registered, it must do so using form BR7.

There is also an obligation to deliver to the Companies Registry, for each branch, particulars relating to any insolvency proceedings involving the foreign company. Forms 703P(1), 703P(3), 703Q(1) and 703Q(2) are prescribed for these purposes, but have not been included.

A company must notify the Companies Registry when it closes a branch. There is no prescribed form.

The above notes merely give an overview. Reference should be made to the detailed provisions if required.

Printed and supplied by

JORDANS
21 St Thomas Street Bristol BS1 6JS
Telephone: 0117 923 0600 Fax: 0117 923 0063

This form must be completed for all
'Place of Business' registrations.
(See note below for re-registration
from a 'Branch')

This form should be completed in black

Return and declaration delivered for registration of a place of business of an oversea company

(Pursuant to section 691 of the Companies Act 1985)

Previous branch number
(if applicable)

| | For official use only |

Company name

Country of incorporation

Address of place of business in Great Britain

Post town _____

County / Region _____

Postcode _____

Either

Constitution of the company

(See notes 1 and 2)
(A certified English translation must be included)

* *Delete as applicable*

\# *Mark appropriate box(es)*

A certified copy of the

\# ☐ Instrument(s) constituting or defining the constitution of the company; and

☐ A certified translation

* is/are delivered for registration

OR

The company must deliver certified copies of its constitutional documents (with certified translations), and the particulars of the company's directors and secretary.
However, if the company is closing a branch registration and effecting a place of business registration, it may rely on the documents or the particulars of the directors and secretary previously filed in that part of Great Britain, provided any relevant alterations to those documents have been updated on the register.

The

\# ☐ The constitutional documents (and a certified translation *)

* and / or

☐ Particulars of the current directors and secretary(ies)

were previously delivered in respect of a branch of the company registered at this registry

Branch Number [＿＿＿＿＿＿＿]

1/93

234

Directors *(See notes 3, 4 and 5)*

Name

*Style/Title   `CD` ⌏

Forenames ⌏

Surname ⌏

*Honours etc ⌏

Previous forenames ⌏

Previous surname ⌏

Address   `AD` ⌏

Usual residential address must be given.
In the case of a corporation, give the
registered or principal office address. ⌏

Post town ⌏

County/Region ⌏

Postcode ⌏ Country ⌏

Date of birth   `DO` ⌏ Nationality `NA` ⌏

(See note 5) Business occupation `OC` ⌏
(if any). If none
other directorships. `OD` ⌏

Name

*Style/Title   `CD` ⌏

Forenames ⌏

Surname ⌏

*Honours etc ⌏

Previous forenames ⌏

Previous surname ⌏

Address   `AD` ⌏

Usual residential address must be given.
In the case of a corporation, give the
registered or principal office address. ⌏

Post town ⌏

County/Region ⌏

Postcode ⌏ Country ⌏

Date of birth   `DO` ⌏ Nationality `NA` ⌏

(See note 5) Business occupation `OC` ⌏
(if any). If none
other directorships. `OD` ⌏

* Voluntary details

Company Secretary(ies)

(See notes 4 and 6)

Name   *Style/Title

                         Forenames

                         Surname

                         *Honours etc

                Previous forenames

                Previous surname

CS

Address

Usual residential address must be given. In the case of a corporation, give the registered or principal office address.

AD

                 Post town

              County/Region

                 Postcode   Country

Name   *Style/Title

                         Forenames

                         Surname

                         *Honours etc

                Previous forenames

                Previous surname

CS

Address

Usual residential address must be given. In the case of a corporation, give the registered or principal office address.

AD

                 Post town

              County/Region

                 Postcode   Country

Person(s) authorised

List of some one or more persons resident in Great Britain authorised to accept on the company's behalf service of process and any notice required to be served on it.

                         *Style/Title

                         Forenames

                         Surname

                         Address

                         Post town

*Voluntary details   County/Region   Postcode

Person(s) authorised (continued)

List of some one or more persons resident in Great Britain authorised to accept on the company's behalf service of process and any notice required to be served on it.

*Style/Title _____

Forenames _____

Surname _____

Address _____

_____

_____

Post town _____

County/Region _____ Postcode _____

---

*Style/Title _____

Forenames _____

Surname _____

Address _____

_____

_____

Post town _____

County/Region _____ Postcode _____

---

*Style/Title _____

Forenames _____

Surname _____

Address _____

_____

_____

Post town _____

County/Region _____ Postcode _____

---

*Style/Title _____

Forenames _____

Surname _____

Address _____

_____

_____

Post town _____

County/Region _____ Postcode _____

*Voluntary details

Declaration *(See note 8)*

Full name and address

I _____

of (address) _____

_____

a †director/†secretary/†person authorised to accept on the company's behalf service of process or any notices required to be served on it, do solemnly and sincerely declare that the company established its place of business in Great Britain on

(enter date)

and I make this solemn declaration conscientiously believing the same to be true and by virtue of the provisions of the Statutory Declarations Act 1835.

Signed _____

Declared at _____

_____

_____

the _____ **day of** _____

one thousand nine hundred and _____

before me _____

A Commissioner for Oaths or Notary Public or Justice of the Peace or Solicitor having the powers conferred on a Commissioner for Oaths. *(See note 8)*

Number of continuation sheets attached

To whom should Companies House direct any enquiries about the information on this form?

_____

_____

_____ Postcode _____

Telephone _____ Extension _____

Please ensure the form is fully completed and then send it to the Registrar of Companies at *(See note 9)*

Companies House, Crown Way, Cardiff CF4 3UZ
for companies establishing a place of business in England and Wales.

Companies House, 100-102 George Street, Edinburgh EH2 3DJ
for companies establishing a place of business in Scotland.

238

Notes

1 The copy of the instrument constituting or defining the constitution of the company must be certified in the place of incorporation of the company to be a true copy:—

    (a) by an official of the Government to whose custody the original is committed; or

    (b) by a notary public; or

    (c) by an officer of the company on oath taken before:

        (i) a person having authority in that place to administer an oath; or

        (ii) any of the British officials mentioned in section 6 of the Commissioners for Oaths Act 1889.

2 The translation of the instrument must be certified to be a correct translation:-

    (a) if the translation was made in the United Kingdom, by

        (i) a notary public in any part of the United Kingdom;

        (ii) a solicitor (if the translation was made in Scotland), a solicitor of the Supreme Court of Judicature of England and Wales (if it was made in England or Wales), or a solicitor of the Supreme Court of Judicature of Northern Ireland (if it was made in Northern Ireland); or

        (iii) a person certified by a person mentioned above to be known to him to be competent to translate the document into English; or

    (b) if the translation was made outside the United Kingdom, by

        (i) a notary public;

        (ii) a person authorised in the place where the translation was made to administer an oath;

        (iii) any of the British officials mentioned in section 6 of the Commissioners for Oaths Act 1889;

        (iv) a person certified by a person mentioned above to be known to him to be competent to translate the document into English.

3 'Director' includes any person who occupies the position of a director, by whatever name called.

4 Show for an individual the full forenames NOT INITIALS and surname together with any previous forenames or surname(s).

If the director or secretary is a corporation or Scottish firm - show the corporate or firm name on the surname line.

Give previous forenames or surname except that:

    · for a married woman, the name by which she was known before marriage need not be given,

    · names not used since the age of 18 or for at least 20 years need not be given.

In the case of a peer, or an individual usually known by a British title, you may state the title instead of or in addition to the forenames and surname and you need not give the name by which that person was known before he or she adopted the title or succeeded to it.

Address:

Give the usual residential address.

In the case of a corporation or Scottish firm give the registered or principal office.

5 In the case of an individual who has a business occupation, this occupation should be named. In the case of an individual who has no business occupation but who holds other directorships, particulars should be given of them.

6 Where all the partners in a firm are joint secretaries, only the firm name and its principal office need be given.

7 Use photocopies of the relevant section(s) of this form to provide details of additional directors, joint secretaries or persons authorised.

8 If made in a foreign country the declaration may be made before any British official mentioned in section 6 of the Commissioners for Oaths Act 1889 or, before any person having authority to administer an oath in that country.

9 If the company establishes a place of business in England and Wales AND in Scotland whether at the same time or not a separate form must be sent to each Registrar.

G

COMPANIES FORM No. 692(1)(a)

Return of alteration in the charter, statutes, etc., of an oversea company

Pursuant to section 692(1)(a) of the Companies Act 1985

Please do not write in this margin

Please complete legibly, preferably in black type, or bold block lettering

* enter corporate name

To the Registrar of Companies

For official use

Company number

Name of company

*

§ insert 'Charter', 'Statutes', 'Memorandum and Articles of Association' or other instrument as the case may be.

Return of alteration in the § _____

_____

constituting or defining the constitution of the above company

Note

A copy of the alteration or a copy of the new deed, if one has been executed, and a translation of the alteration or deed if not in the English language must accompany this return. The actual documents enclosed should be listed below.

† delete as appropriate

Signed _____ [Director][Secretary][Person Authorised]† Date

Note

The time within which this return is to be delivered to the registrar is 21 days after the date on which notice of the alteration in question could have been received in Great Britain in due course of post (if despatched with due diligence).

Presentor's name address and reference (if any):

For official Use
New Companies Section   Post room

JORDANS

2.89

Supplied by Jordans Limited   Tel. 0117 923 0600

Printed and supplied by

JORDANS
21 St Thomas Street Bristol BS1 6JS
Telephone: 0117 923 0600   Fax: 0117 923 0063

692(1)(b)

Return of alteration in the directors or secretary of an oversea company or in their particulars.

This form should be completed in black.

Company number **CN**

Company name

Appointment

(Turn over page for resignation and change of particulars).

	Day	Month	Year
Date of appointment	**DA**		

Appointment of director **CD**

Appointment of secretary **CS**

Please mark the appropriate box.
If appointment is as a director and secretary
mark both boxes.

Name   *Style/title

Forenames

Surname

*Honours etc

Previous forenames

Previous surname

Usual residential address   **AD**

NOTES

Show the full forenames. **NOT INITIALS**
If the director or secretary is a
Corporation or Scottish firm, show
the name on surname line and
registered or principal office on the
usual residential address line.

Give previous forenames or surname
except:
- for a married woman the name before
  marriage need not be given.
- for names not used since the age of 18
  or for at least 20 years.
A peer or individual known by a title
may state the title instead of or in
addition to the forenames and surname.

Post town

County/region

Postcode   Country

Date of birth†   **DO**   Nationality† **NA**

In the case of an individual who
has no business occupation but
holds other directorships, give
particulars of them.

Business occupation†
(if any). If none
other directorships.   **OC**

OD

*Voluntary details   †Directors only

A serving director etc must also sign the form overleaf.

Resignation

(This includes any
form of ceasing to
hold office e.g.
death or removal
from office).

Date of resignation etc

DR ☐ ☐ ☐

Resignation etc, as director

XD ☐

Resignation etc, as secretary

XS ☐

Please mark the appropriate box.
If resignation etc is as a director and secretary
mark both boxes.

Forenames

_____

Surname

_____

Date of birth *(directors only)*

DO ☐ ☐ ☐

If cessation is other than resignation, please state reason
(eg death)

Change of particulars

*Complete this section
in all cases where
particulars have
changed and then the
appropriate section
below.*

Date of change of particulars

DC ☐ ☐ ☐

Change of particulars, as director

ZD ☐

Change of particulars, as secretary

ZS ☐

Please mark the appropriate box.
If change of particulars is as a director and secretary
mark both boxes.

Forenames

Surname

*(name previously
notified to
Companies House)*

_____

Date of birth *(directors only)*

DO ☐ ☐ ☐

Change of name *(enter new name)* Forenames

NN _____

Surname

_____

Change of usual residential address *(enter new address)*

AD _____

_____

_____

Post town

_____

County/region

_____

Postcode _____ Country _____

Other change *(please specify)*

_____

**A serving director/secretary/person authorised must sign
the form below.**

Signature

Signed _____ Dated _____

Director/Secretary/Person Authorised *(Delete as appropriate)*

After signing please return the form to the Registrar
of Companies at

*If the company establishes a place of business both in
England and Wales and in Scotland a separate form
must be sent to each Registrar.*

or

Companies House, Crown Way, Cardiff CF4 3UZ
for companies registered in England and Wales
Companies House, 100-102 George Street, Edinburgh EH2 3DJ
for companies registered in Scotland.

To whom should Companies House direct any
enquiries about the information on this form?

_____

_____

_____ Tel: _____

COMPANIES FORM No. 692(1)(c)

Return of alteration in the names or addresses of persons resident in Great Britain authorised to accept service on behalf of an oversea company

692(1)(c)

Pursuant to section 692(1)(c) of the Companies Act 1985

Note: The time within which a return containing the particulars of alteration is to be delivered to the Registrar is twenty one days after the making of such alterations.

To the Registrar of Companies

For official use

Company number

Name of company

*

notifies you of the following alteration(s) in the name(s) or address(es) of persons resident in Great Britain authorised to accept service on behalf of the company

Signed   [Director][Secretary][Person Authorised]† Date

Presentor's name address and reference (if any):

For official Use

General Section   Post room

Supplied by Jordans Limited   Tel. 0117 923 0600

G

COMPANIES FORM No. 692(2)

Return of change in the corporate name of an oversea company

Note: this form should be used where name changed is name in country of incorporation

Please do not write in this margin

Pursuant to section 692(2) of the Companies Act 1985

Please complete legibly, preferably in black type, or bold block lettering

To the Registrar of Companies

For official use   Company number

* enter name registered in Great Britain

Name of company

*

Particulars of change of name

1. Old corporate name

2. New corporate name

3. Date of change of corporate name

† delete as appropriate

Signed _____   [Director][Secretary][Person Authorised]† Date

Presentor's name address and reference (if any):

For official Use
General Section   Post room

JORDANS

2.89

Supplied by Jordans Limited   Tel. 0117 923 0600

BR1

This form should be completed in black.

Return delivered for registration of a branch of an oversea company

(Pursuant to Schedule 21A, paragraph 1 of the Companies Act 1985)

For office use only	CN		BN	

Corporate name
(name in parent state)
(See note 5)

Business name
(if different to corporate name)

Country of incorporation

Identity of register
(if applicable)

and registration no. _____

Legal form
(See note 3)

1 See note 2

PART A - COMPANY DETAILS 1

* State whether the company is
a credit or financial institution

* Is the company subject to Section 699A of the Companies Act 1985?

YES ☐   NO ☐

(1) These boxes need not be completed by companies formed in EC member states

Governing law
(See note 4)

Accounting requirements

Period for which the company is required to prepare accounts by parent law.   from _____ to _____

Period allowed for the preparation and public disclosure of accounts for the above period _____ months

248

(2) This Box need NOT be completed by companies from EC member states, OR where the constitutional documents of the company already show this information.

Address of principal place of business in home country

_____

_____

Objects of company

_____

Issued share capital

_____ Currency _____

Company Secretary(ies)
(See note 10)

Name

*Voluntary details

* Style/Title _____

Forenames _____

Surname _____

* Honours etc. _____

Previous Forenames _____

Previous surname _____

Address

_____

_____

Usual residential address must be given. In the case of a corporation, give the registered or principal office address.

Post town _____

County/Region _____

Postcode _____ Country_____

Company Secretary(ies)
(See note 10)

Name

*Voluntary details

* Style/Title _____

Forenames _____

Surname _____

* Honours etc. _____

Previous Forenames _____

Previous surname _____

Address

_____

_____

Usual residential address must be given. In the case of a corporation, give the registered or principal office address.

Post town _____

County/Region _____

Postcode _____ Country_____

(You may photocopy this page if required)

Directors
(See note 10)

Name

* Voluntary details

Address

Usual residential address must be given. In the case of a corporation, give the registered or principal office address.

SCOPE OF AUTHORITY

Give brief particulars of the extent of the powers exercised. (e.g. whether they are limited to powers expressly conferred by the instrument of appointment; or whether they are subject to express limitations.) Where the powers are exercised jointly give the name(s) of the person(s) concerned. You may cross refer to the details of person(s) disclosed elsewhere on the form.

‡ Mark box(es) as applicable.

(You may photocopy this page as required)

* Style/Title _____

Forenames _____

Surname _____

* Honours etc. _____

Previous Forenames _____

Previous surname _____

_____

_____

Post town _____

County/Region _____

Postcode _____ Country _____

Date of Birth [| |] Nationality _____

Business Occupation _____

Other Directorships _____

_____

_____

The extent of the authority to represent the company is :- (give details)

_____

_____

_____

_____

_____

These powers :-

‡ ☐ May be exercised alone

OR

‡ ☐ Must be exercised with :-
(Give name(s) of co-authorised person(s))

_____

_____

_____

_____

250

Directors

(See note 10)

Name

* Voluntary details

Address

Usual residential address must be given. In the case of a corporation, give the registered or principal office address.

SCOPE OF AUTHORITY

Give brief particulars of the extent of the powers exercised. (e.g. whether they are limited to powers expressly conferred by the instrument of appointment; or whether they are bject to express limitations.)
Where the powers are exercised jointly give the name(s) of the person(s) concerned. You may cross refer to the details of person(s) disclosed elsewhere on the form.

‡ Mark box(es) as applicable.

(You may photocopy this page as required)

* Style/Title _____

Forenames _____

Surname _____

* Honours etc. _____

Previous Forenames _____

Previous surname _____

_____

_____

Post town _____

County/Region _____

Postcode _____   Country_____

Date of Birth [| | |]   Nationality_____

Business Occupation _____

Other Directorships _____

_____

_____

The extent of the authority to represent the company is :- (give details)

_____

_____

_____

_____

_____

These powers :-

‡ ☐   May be exercised alone
OR

‡ ☐   Must be exercised with :-
          (Give name(s) of co-authorised person(s))

_____

_____

_____

_____

Constitution of company
(See notes 6 to 9)

\# Mark box(es)
as applicable

(See note 9)

* Delete as applicable

\# ☐ A certified copy of the instrument constituting or defining the constitution of the company

AND

☐ * A certified translation

* is/are delivered for registration

AND/OR

A certified copy of the constitutional documents and latest accounts of the company, together with a certified translation of them if they are not in the English language, must accompany this form.

\# ☐ A copy of the latest accounts of the company

AND

☐ A certified translation

* is/are delivered for registration

AND/OR

The company may rely on constitutional and accounting documents previously filed in respect of another branch registered in the United Kingdom.

The

\# ☐ Constitutional documents (* and certified translations)

AND/OR

☐ The latest accounts (* and certified translations)

of the company were previously delivered on the registration of the branch or the company at :-

Cardiff ☐ Edinburgh ☐ Belfast ☐

Registration no. [_____]

AND/OR

The company may also rely on particulars about the company previously filed in respect of another branch in that part of Great Britain, provided that any alterations have been notified to the Registrar.

☐ the particulars about the company were previously delivered in respect of a branch of the company registered at THIS registry.

Registration no. [_____]

AND/OR

The company may also rely on constitutional documents and particulars about the company officers previously filed in respect of a former Place of Business of that company, provided that any alterations have been notified to the Registrar.

NOTE :- In all cases, the registration number of the branch or place of business relied upon must be given.

The

☐ Constitutional documents (* and certified translations)

AND/OR

☐ Particulars of the current directors and secretary(s)

were previously delivered in respect of a place of business of the company registered at THIS registry.

Registration no. [_____]

PART B - BRANCH DETAILS

Persons authorised to represent the company or accept service of process.

Give details of all persons who are authorised to represent the company as permanent representatives of the company in respect of the business of the branch.
Give details also of all persons resident in Great Britain, who are authorised to accept service or process on the company's behalf.

* Delete as appropriate

SCOPE OF AUTHORITY

(This part does not apply to a person only authorised to accept service on behalf of the company)

Give brief particulars of the extent of the powers exercised. (e.g. whether they are limited to powers expressly conferred by the instrument of appointment; or whether they are subject to express limitations.) Where the powers are exercised jointly give the name(s) of the person(s) concerned. You may cross refer to the details of person(s) disclosed elsewhere on the form.

‡ Mark box(es) as appropriate

---

* Style/Title _____

Forenames _____

Surname _____

Address _____

_____

Post town _____

County/Region _____ Postcode _____

Is ‡ ☐ Authorised to accept service of process on the company's behalf

* AND/OR

Is ‡ ☐ Authorised to represent the company in relation to that business
The extent of the authority to represent the company is :- (give details)

_____

_____

_____

_____

_____

These powers :-

‡ ☐ May be exercised alone

OR

‡ ☐ Must be exercised with :-
      (Give name(s) of co-authorised person(s))

_____

_____

_____

_____

Persons authorised to represent the company or accept service of process.

Give details of all persons who are authorised to represent the company as permanent representatives of the company in respect of the business of the branch.
Give details also of all persons resident in Great Britain, who are authorised to accept service or process on the company's behalf.

* Delete as appropriate

SCOPE OF AUTHORITY

(This part does not apply to a person only authorised to accept service on behalf of the company)

Give brief particulars of the extent of the powers exercised. (e.g. whether they are limited to powers expressly conferred by the instrument of appointment; or whether they are subject to express limitations.)
Where the powers are exercised, jointly give the name(s) of the person(s) concerned. You may cross refer to the details of person(s) disclosed elsewhere on the form.

‡ Mark box(es) as appropriate

(You may photocopy this page as required)

---

* Style/Title _____

Forenames _____

Surname _____

Address _____

_____

Post town _____

County/Region _____ Postcode _____

Is ‡ ☐ Authorised to accept service of process on the company's behalf

* AND/OR

Is ‡ ☐ Authorised to represent the company in relation to that business

The extent of the authority to represent the company is :- (give details)

_____

_____

_____

_____

_____

These powers :-

‡ ☐ May be exercised alone

OR

‡ ☐ Must be exercised with :-
   (Give name(s) of co-authorised person(s))

_____

_____

_____

_____

254

Address of branch
(See note 11)

Address _____

_____

Post town _____

County/Region _____ Postcode _____

Branch details
(See note 12)

Date branch opened

Business carried on at branch _____

_____

_____

_____

SIGNATURE

Signed _____
(* Director / Secretary / Permanent representative)

Date _____

This form contains...........................continuation sheets.

To whom should Companies House direct any enquiries about the information on this form?

Name _____

Address _____

_____

_____ Postcode _____

Telephone _____ Extension _____

When completed, this form together with any enclosures should be delivered to the Registrar of Companies at

for branches established in England and Wales

**Companies House
Crown Way
Cardiff
CF4 3UZ**

for branches established in Scotland

**Companies House
100 - 102 George Street
Edinburgh
EH2 3DJ**

NOTES

Read these notes carefully before completing the form

1. Registration requirement

Every oversea company setting up a place of business in Great Britain must register with the appropriate registry of the jurisdiction in which the place of business is situated. (For further guidance please refer to the Companies House notes on "Oversea Companies")

If a Place of Business" is being established then FORM 691 must be used: if a branch is being registered then THIS FORM must be used.

A company must register all of its branches.

The requirement to register applies to any limited company which is incorporated outside the United Kingdom and which establishes a branch in Great Britain. Northern Ireland companies, being within the UK, are not required to register any branches in Great Britain. They are, however, required to register as having a place of business by submitting form 691 when they set up business in Great Britain.

2. Completion of Form BR1

If this is the first registration of a branch of an oversea company in the UK, ALL the relevant details of the form must be completed. If a previous branch of the company has already been registered in the UK, and has not closed, registration of the second and any subsequent branches need not complete Part A (Company details) (provided any alterations to those details have been updated), but must complete part B (Branch details).

The forms should be delivered to the relevant Registrar with supporting documents within 1 month of having opened the branch.

3. "Legal Form"

The details of the company's legal form must be disclosed. This includes whether the company is a private or public company, whether it is limited, and, if so, the manner of limitation.

4. "Governing Law"

A company which is not incorporated in an EC member state must state the law under which it is incorporated. This means the relevant rules or legislation which regulate the incorporation of companies in that state: e.g. "Companies Act of (state) 19XX"

5. Names

An oversea company wishing to register its corporate name is subject to the same regulations as British companies. Accordingly, any name which an oversea company wishes to use may be unacceptable or only permissible with the approval of the Secretary of State. A company which is served a notice to this effect may then complete form 694(4)(a) giving another name, approved by the Secretary of State, under which it proposes carrying on business in Great Britain.

6. Delivery of documents in respect of more than one branch.

If the constitutional documents and last accounts of the company have been delivered in respect of another branch in the UK, prior to registration of this branch, the company may rely on these deliveries rather than delivering another set of documents. The company must mark the appropriate boxes, stating the branch in respect of which those documents have already been delivered, the branch number, and the place at which they were registered.

If the company particulars have been delivered in respect of another branch of the company in THE SAME PART of Great Britain prior to registration of this branch (and any alterations have been updated), the company may rely on this delivery, rather than re-disclosing the particulars on this form.

7. Delivery of documents where previous place of business has been registered.

Where the constitutional documents, and the particulars of the directors and secretary(ies) have been delivered in respect of a former place of business in THE SAME PART of Great Britain (and changes to those documents or particulars have been updated), the company may rely on those deliveries rather than re-delivering the documents or re-disclosing those particulars in respect of the branch.

8. Certification of constitutional documents.

A copy of the document(s) constituting or defining the company must be certified in the place of incorporation to be a true copy by:

(a) an official of the Government in whose custody the original is committed; or

(b) a notary public; or

(c) an officer of the company on oath taken before

(i) a person having authority in that place to administer an oath; or

(ii) any of the British officials mentioned in section 6 of the Commissioners for Oaths Act 1889.

9. Translations

If the constitutional documents of the company or the latest accounts and reports are not written in the English language, they must be accompanied by a certified translation. This must be done in the following manner:

(a) If the translation is made in the United Kingdom, by:

(i) a notary public in any part of the United Kingdom;

(ii) a solicitor (if the translation was made in Scotland), a solicitor of the Supreme Court of Judicature of England and Wales (if it was made in England or Wales), or a solicitor of the Supreme Court of Judicature of Northern Ireland (if it was made in Northern Ireland); or

(iii) a person certified by a person mentioned above to be known to him to be competent to translate the document into English; or

Notes (continued)

(b) if the translation was made outside the United Kingdom, by

    (i) a notary public;

    (ii) a person authorised in the place where the translation was made to administer an oath;

    (iii) any of the British officials mentioned in section 6 of the Commissioners for Oaths Act 1889;

    (iv) a person certified by a person mentioned above known to him to be competent to translate the document into English.

10. Directors and secretary's details

"Director" includes any person who occupies the position of director regardless of what name he is called.

For an individual, show the full names, NOT INITIALS, together with any previous names. However, previous names need not be given in the case of

- a married woman, the name by which she was known prior to marriage;

- any former name which has been changed or disused since the age of 18, OR for at least 20 years;

- a peer, or an individual normally known by a title, you may state that title instead of the name by which that person was known before adopting the title.

If the director or secretary is a corporation or Scottish firm, show the corporate or firm name on the surname line.

Addresses

Give the usual residential address

In the case of a corporation or Scottish firm, give the registered or principal office address.

11. Branch Address

Give the address of the principal place of business of the branch. For branches registering in England and Wales, this address must be in England or Wales. For branches registering in Scotland, this address must be in Scotland.

12. Business and Date of commencement.

State the date on which the branch was opened and give brief details of the business of the branch.

13. Photocopies

If there is insufficient space on the form for details about directors, secretaries or permanent representatives, you may photocopy the appropriate pages.

14. Completion of form.

The completed form should be signed by an officer or permanent representative of the company and delivered to the appropriate Registrar, together with any supporting documents within one month of the branch being established.

15. Delivery of winding-up, insolvency etc. particulars.

If, at any time prior to the registration in Great Britain of the first branch of an oversea company, the company has become subject to winding up, insolvency or similar proceedings, and remains subject to those proceedings, the company must at the same time as delivering Form BR1, also deliver Form 703P(1), 703P(3), 703Q(1) (as appropriate). For further details on these forms please see the Companies House Notes for Guidance on Oversea Companies.

BR2

This form should be completed in black.

Return by an oversea company subject to branch registration of an alteration to constitutional documents
(Pursuant to Schedule 21A, paragraph 7(1) of the Companies Act 1985)

Company number

Company name

Branch number

Branch Name

CONSTITUTIONAL DOCUMENTS

On [   ] an alteration was made to the

constitutional document(s) of the company

A copy of the new instrument is attached

* A certified translation is also attached

* Delete as applicable

Note.:- A company is only required to make a return in respect of a branch where the document altered is included amongst the material registered in respect of that branch

Signed _____
*   Director/Secretary/Permanent representative

Date _____

When completed, this form should be returned to the address overleaf

To whom should Companies House direct any enquiries about the information on this form

Name _____

Address _____

_____

_____ Telephone no. _____

When completed, this form should be delivered to :-

For branches registered in England and Wales	For branches registered in Scotland
The Registrar of Companies Companies House Crown Way Cardiff CF4 3UZ	The Registrar of Companies Companies House 100 - 102 George Street Edinburgh EH2 3DJ

Printed and supplied by

JORDANS
21 St Thomas Street Bristol BS1 6JS
Telephone: 0117 923 0600   Fax: 0117 923 0063

BR3

This form should be completed in black.

Return by an oversea company subject to branch registration, for alteration of company particulars

(Pursuant to Schedule 21A, paragraph 7(1) of the Companies Act 1985)

Company number

Company name

(See note 1 on Page 3)   Branch name
(if different to company name)

Particulars of change

1. Change of name

Note: If the company has changed its corporate name in its country of origin, give details here together with the date the change was registered or otherwise made.

Old corporate name

New corporate name

Date of change

2. Change in legal form
(Give details of change)

Note: If the company has changed its legal form either by its own decision or by a change in its parent law, give details here

Date of change

3. Change to accounting requirements

Period for which the company is required to prepare accounts by parent law, in substitution for a period previously notified, has been changed to:

(dates) _____ to _____

Period allowed for the preparation and public disclosure of accounts for the above period

_____ months

260

Company Particulars

NOTE. The changes to items 3 - 7 only are not required to be notified by companies incorporated in an EC member state or if the changes are already disclosed in the constitutional documents which have been filed with the Registrar.

4. Principal address

On* _____ the company changed its principal address
in its parent state to

(give new principal
place of business)

_____

_____

_____

* insert date of change

_____

5. Objects

On* _____ the company changed its objects to those
†described below/attached

(state new objects)

_____

_____

_____

† delete as applicable

_____

6. Capital

On* _____ **the company increased/decreased its
issued share capital from** _____ **to** _____

(state new issued share
capital (incl. currency))

7. Governing law

List any change in the law
under which the company was
incorporated (e.g. a new Act)
include the date of the change.

_____

_____

Date _____

When completed, this form should be signed overleaf and returned to :-

For branches registered in England and Wales

**The Registrar of Companies
Companies House
Crown Way
Cardiff
CF4 3UZ**

For branches registered in Scotland

**The Registrar of Companies
Companies House
100 - 102 George Street
Edinburgh
EH2 3DJ**

261

Form BR3

To whom should
Companies House
direct any enquiries
regarding this form

Name	
Address	
	Tel. No

* Delete as applicable

This return is delivered in respect of all the branches listed below, registered at * Cardiff / Edinburgh.

This notice must be delivered
to the Registrar within 21 days
of the notice of the alteration
being received in Great Britain
in due course of post (if
despatched with due diligence)

Signed _____

(* Director / Secretary / Permanent representative)

Date _____

Registration number	Branch name

NOTE:- A return must be delivered in respect of any alteration to the company particulars by each branch of an oversea company. If, however, a company has more than one branch in THE SAME PART of Great Britain, it may deliver only one form in respect of all those branches, provided it completes the table above on this page.

Printed and supplied by

JORDANS
21 St Thomas Street Bristol BS1 6JS
Telephone: 0117 923 0600 Fax: 0117 923 0063

BR4

This form should be completed in black.

Return by an oversea company subject to branch registration of change of directors or secretary or of their particulars

(Pursuant to Schedule 21A, paragraph 7(1) of the Companies Act 1985)

Company number

Branch number

Company name

Branch name
(if different)

Resignation, etc.

(This includes any form of ceasing to hold office e.g. death or removal from office)

Date of resignation etc

DR

Resignation etc, as director

XD

Resignation etc, as secretary

XS

Please mark the appropriate box.
If resignation etc is as a director and secretary mark both boxes

Forenames

Surname

Date of birth (directors only)

DO

(See note on page 4)

To whom should Companies House address any enquiries about the information on this form

This return is delivered in respect of all the branches listed on page 4

Name

Address

Telephone

When completed, this form should be returned to the address on page 4

264

Appointment

(Turn to page 3
notify resignation
or alteration of
particulars)

Notes
Show the full forenames **NOT
INITIALS**. If the director or
secretary is a corporation or Scottish
firm, show the name on surname line
and registered or principal office on the
usual residential address line

Give previous forenames or surnames
except:
-for a married woman the name before
marriage need not be given.
-for names not used since the age of 18
or for at least 20 years.
A peer or individual known by a title
may state the title instead of or in
addition to the forenames and surnames

* Voluntary details
† Directors only

Other directorships
Give the name of every company
incorporated in Great Britain
which the person concerned is a
director or has been a director at any
time in the past 5 years. Exclude a
company which either is, or at all
times during the past 5 years when
the person was a director, was

-dormant
-a parent company which wholly
owned the company making the
return
-another wholly owned subsidiary
of the same parent company

You may use a separate sheet of
paper if necessary.

Give brief particulars of the extent of the
powers exercised (e.g. whether they are
limited to powers expressly conferred by
the instrument of appointment, or whether
they are subject to express limitations).
Where the powers are exercised jointly,
give the name(s) of the person(s)

‡ Mark as applicable

This return must be delivered to
the Registrar within 21 days of
the notice being received in
Great Britain in due course of
post (if despatched with due
diligence)

Date of appointment	DA
Appointment of director	CD } Please mark the appropriate box. If appointment is as a director and secretary mark both boxes.
Appointment of secretary	CS
Name *Style/title	
Forenames	
Surname	
*Honours etc	
Previous forenames	
Previous surname	
Usual residential address	AD
Post town	
County/region	
Postcode	
† Date of birth	DO † Nationality NA
† Business Occupation	OC
† Other directorships	

Scope of authority   The extent of the authority to represent the company is
(give details)

These powers:

‡ ☐   May be exercised acting alone,

‡ ☐   Must be exercised with :- (give names of
co-authorised person(s))

I consent to act as director/secretary of the above named company

Consent signature   Signed _____ Date _____

A serving director etc must also sign the form on page 4

ALTERATION OF PARTICULARS

(this section is not for appointments or resignations)

Complete this section in all cases where particulars of a serving director/secretary have changed and then the appropriate section below

Date of change of particulars

Change of particulars, as director

Change of particulars, as secretary

Forenames (name previously notified to Companies House)

Surname

Date of birth (directors only)

Change of name (enter new name)   Forenames

Surname

Change of usual residential address (enter new address)

Post town

County/region

Postcode

Nationality

Change to authority to act (if applicable)

Give brief particulars of any change in the authority of a director to represent the company, including any alteration to the manner in which existing or new powers may be exercised (e.g. requiring them to be exercised with other persons.)

\#   Mark as applicable

DR

XD   { Please mark the appropriate box. If change of particulars is as a director and secretary mark both boxes

XS

DO

AD

Country

The extent of the authority of the above person to represent the company has been altered to :- (give details)

These powers:

\# ☐   May be exercised alone, or

\# ☐   Must be exercised with : (give names of co-authorised persons)

266

Registration number	Branch name

NOTE :- A return must be delivered in respect of any alteration to the company particulars by each branch of an oversea company. If, however, a company has more than one branch in THE SAME PART of Great Britain, it may deliver only one form in respect of all those branches, provided it completes the table above on this page.

When completed, this form should be delivered to :-

For branches registered in England and Wales

For branches registered in Scotland

The Registrar of Companies
Companies House
Crown Way
Cardiff
CF4 3UZ

The Registrar of Companies
Companies House
100 - 102 George Street
Edinburgh
EH2 3DJ

BR5

Return by an oversea company subject to branch registration of change of address or other branch particulars

(Pursuant to Schedule 21A, paragraph 7(1) of the Companies Act 1985)

This form should be completed in black.

Company number	Branch number
Corporate name	
Branch name (if applicable)	

Change of Address

Previous address of branch

This return must be delivered to the Registrar within 21 days of the alteration being made.

RO _____

_____

Post town _____

County/Region _____

Postcode _____

* Delete as applicable

*   England/Wales   Scotland

New address of branch

N.B. If a company moves a branch from one part of the United Kingdom to another part of the United Kingdom then it must close its registration in the first part (notifying the Registrar) and re-register the branch at the new registry.

RO _____

_____

Post town _____

County/Region _____

Postcode _____

* Delete as applicable

*   England/Wales   Scotland

Date of change [| | |]

Change in nature of business carried on at the branch

(Describe new business)

_____
_____
_____
_____

Date of change [| | |]

See overleaf for other branch changes

268

**Change of business name
of the branch**

Previous name _____

New name _____

_____

Date of change ☐|☐|☐|☐

Signature   Signed _____
                        * Director / Secretary / Permanent representative

                 Date _____

To whom should Companies
House address any enquiries
about the information on this
form

_____

_____

_____

_____ Tel _____

When completed, this form should be delivered to

for branches registered in England and Wales   or for branches registered in Scotland

The Registrar of Companies   The Registrar of Companies
Companies House   Companies House
Crown Way   100 - 102 George Street
Cardiff   Edinburgh
CF4 3UZ   EH2 3DJ

1 93

BR6

This form should be completed in black.

This notice must be delivered to the Registrar within 21 days of the alteration being made.

Return of change of person authorised to accept service or to represent the branch of an oversea company or of any change in their particulars

(Pursuant to Schedule 21A, paragraph 7(1) of the Companies Act 1985)

Company number

Branch number

Company name

Branch name
(If different to corporate name)

TERMINATION OF AUTHORITY

See overleaf for appointments and change of particulars

Date of termination

Position vacated
(Mark appropriate box(es))

☐ Person authorised to accept service on the company's behalf

☐ Person authorised to represent the company at the branch

Complete these details for resignation of any person authorised to accept service or process on the company's behalf or who was authorised to represent the company in relation to the business of the branch.

Name

Address

To whom should Companies House direct any enquiries about the information on this form

Tel.

When completed, this form should be delivered to the address on page 4

270

APPOINTMENT

Persons authorised to represent the company or who may accept service or process

Give the name and address of the person appointed, together with the date of appointment. Mark the box(es) relevant to the appointment. If the appointment is to both positions mark both boxes.

* Delete as appropriate.

---

*Style/Title _____

Forenames _____

Surname _____

Address _____

_____

County/Region _____ Postcode _____

☐   Is authorised to accept service of process on the company's behalf

* AND/OR

☐   Is authorised to represent the company in relation to that business

Date of appointment | | | |

SCOPE OF AUTHORITY

The authority to represent the company is :-

Is # ☐   Authorised to accept service of process on the company's behalf

* AND/OR

Is # ☐   Authorised to represent the company in relation to that business

The extent of the authority to represent the company is :- (give details)

Give brief particulars of the extent of the powers exercised. (e.g. whether they are limited to powers expressly conferred by the instrument of appointment; or whether they are subject to express limitations.) Where the powers are exercised, jointly give the name(s) of the person(s) concerned.

_____

_____

_____

_____

_____

These powers :-

☐   May be exercised alone

OR

Mark box(es) as appropriate.

☐   Must be exercised with :-

       (Give name(s) of co-authorised person(s))

_____

_____

_____

_____

CHANGE OF PARTICULARS

Mark the appropriate box. If change relates to both positions, mark both boxes

Date of change

☐ Change of particulars of person authorised to accept service

☐ Change of particulars of person authorised to represent the company

Change of name

Name previously notified to Companies House

Forenames _____

Surname _____

New name

Forenames _____

Surname _____

Change of residential address

(enter new address)

Address _____

_____

Post town _____

County/Region _____ Postcode _____

Country _____

Change of authority to act

(this part does not apply to a person authorised to accept service on behalf of the company)

Give brief particulars of any change in the authority of the officer to represent the company, including any alteration to the manner in which the existing or new powers may be exercised (e.g. requiring them to be exercised with other persons)

The extent of the authority of the above person to represent the company has been altered to :- [give details]

_____

_____

_____

_____

The powers :

☐ May be exercised alone

or

Mark appropriate box

☐ Must be exercised with : [give names of co-authorised person(s)]

_____

_____

_____

_____

Signature

Signed _____

* Director / Secretary / Permanent representative

* Delete as applicable

Date _____

Form BR6

When completed, this form should be delivered to :-

For branches registered in England and Wales

The Registrar of Companies
Companies House
Crown Way
Cardiff
CF4 3UZ

For branches registered in Scotland

The Registrar of Companies
Companies House
100 - 102 George Street
Edinburgh
EH2 3DJ

1/93

BR7

This form should be completed in black.

Return by an oversea company of the branch at which the constitutional documents of the company have been registered in substitution for a previous branch

(Pursuant to Schedule 21A, paragraph 8(2) of the Companies Act 1985)

Company number

Company name

If this form is delivered in respect of other branches in the same part of Great Britain, list the branch numbers overleaf.

Gives notice that the :-

\# ☐ Constitutional documents of the company

* ☐ A certified translation

are now included in the documents which are registered in respect of another branch

* Delete as applicable

Mark appropriate boxes

Registered number of that branch

Place of registration

\# **Cardiff** ☐   **Edinburgh** ☐   **Belfast** ☐

This return must be delivered to the Registrar within 21 days of the notice of the alteration being received in Great Britain in due course of post (if despatched with due diligence)

Signed _____
　　　　　* Director / Secretary / Permanent representative

Date _____

This form is delivered in respect of all the branches listed overleaf

To whom should Companies House direct any enquiries about the information on this form

Tel.

274

Registration number	Branch name

When completed, this form should be delivered to :-

For branches registered in England and Wales

The Registrar of Companies
Companies House
Crown Way
Cardiff
CF4 3UZ

For branches registered in Scotland

The Registrar of Companies
Companies House
100 - 102 George Street
Edinburgh
EH2 3DJ